For Robert E. Hoover
of Wantagh Baptist Church and
Carl Kammeraad and
Duane Kelderman of
Neland Avenue Christian Reformed Church,
who tell the story of the Bible

—G.S.

For Buffy Rich

—D.N.

STORIES FROM THE OLD
AND NEW TESTAMENTS
RETOLD BY

Gary D. Schmidt

ILLUSTRATED BY

Dennis Nolan

The
Blessing
of the
Lord

WILLIAM B. EERDMANS PUBLISHING COMPANY
Grand Rapids, Michigan — Cambridge, U. K.

Text copyright © 1997 by Gary D. Schmidt
Illustrations copyright © 1997 by Dennis Nolan
Published by Eerdmans Books for Young Readers
an imprint of Wm. B. Eerdmans Publishing Co.
255 Jefferson Ave. S.E., Grand Rapids, Michigan 49503
P.O. Box 163, Cambridge   CB3 9PU U.K.

Printed in Hong Kong
00 99 98 97   7 6 5 4 3 2 1

Library of Congress Cataloging-in-Publication Data
Schmidt, Gary D.
The blessing of the Lord : stories from the Old and New
Testaments / by Gary D. Schmidt.
p.   cm.
Summary: Retells twenty-five Bible stories, exploring the point of
view of the characters in each story.
ISBN 0-8028-3789-1 (alk. paper)
1. Bible stories, English.   [1. Bible stories.]   I. Title.
* BS551.2.S37   1997*
*   220.9'505—dc20   96-11402*
*   CIP*
*   AC*

The illustrations were rendered in watercolor.
The text type is set in Galliard.
The display type is set in Goudy Old Style.
The book was designed by Joy Chu.

CONTENTS

Stories from the New Testament

I remember a set of pictures that Mrs. Chicola held up whenever she told stories from the Bible. In one, Goliath was falling dramatically backwards while David hadn't yet finished with his follow-through. In another, Daniel sat bathed in a beam of sunlight while the lions slept around him. Adam and Eve roamed Eden, accompanied by lambs and lions, while Samson pushed down the pillars of the temple of Dagon, throwing panic and confusion into the gaudily clad worshippers.

Sitting on the black-tiled floor in the severe Quaker Meeting House behind the church, I took those stories in as avidly as the milk and cookies that followed them. Mrs. Chicola — and the others who taught me in my progression from room to room in the old Meeting House — told the stories as if they were the most important stories in the world, as if they were more real in some ways than life outside the Meeting House. And in some ways they were.

Even then, though, I can remember feeling some distance from these characters. Moses, Gideon, Elijah, Daniel, Peter — they all seemed a bit daunting, and I wasn't quite sure that I was eager to meet them. I wondered what others who had known them felt about them. And I wondered what others on the edges of their stories thought about their experiences. What must the sons of Leah have felt when Jacob so clearly favored the sons of Rachel? What must Elisha have felt when he lost Elijah, even though Elijah went up to heaven in a storm of fire? What must Purah have thought when he was walking behind Gideon in the midst of thousands of Midianites all ready to kill him? What must Abraham and Mary have thought when confronted by an angel of the Lord? Did Noah become discouraged? Was Ananias confused? Was the centurion at Calvary surprised?

The Bible answers none of these questions. Its stories are bold and sweeping, capturing the lives of figures caught up in God's story. But at the same time, the stories are about human characters, not demi-gods, who make mistakes, who are faithful, who are fearful, who walk with the knowledge of God's hand upon them, who try to test God, who fail, who learn.

So these stories are the product of three decades of thinking about these very human characters caught up in extraordinary events. Each of the stories is set in a moment of crisis, when human frailty comes face to face with God Almighty, and when through grace God teaches and cajoles and leads to Himself. Some of the stories are told by characters on the periphery, who see God's hand but cannot understand it. Others are told by characters who see that same hand and respond in love and faith.

The stories follow the spreading blessing of the Lord. The blessing given to one man — Abraham — is in turn given to one family, and from there to one nation, working itself out in ways that Abraham could never have anticipated. From there, the blessing comes from one nation to all nations of the world, beginning in this collection with the centurion at Calvary. The stories conclude with Saul, soon to be called Paul, who will bring the blessing of the Lord to those who have never heard the story and who live very far away from the land of Jesus.

If the stories begin in the middle of a crisis, they often end before everything is resolved. Many of the Bible's stories are like this, it seems to me — pointing, pushing, shoving us along, but never fully finished and at rest in this world. Rest, suggests George Herbert, is one of the treasures of God, but not one that He lightly bestows. All God's other treasures we keep "with repining restlessness," so that "If goodness lead [us] not, yet weariness/May toss [us] to [His] breast." These are stories of those who seek the rest of God, and who find the road to it in the most surprising places.

Gary D. Schmidt

Stories from the Old Testament

Eve AT THE TREE OF THE KNOWLEDGE OF GOOD AND EVIL

In all the world that God had created, there were no other creatures like Adam and Eve. They delighted God. In the cool dawn, in the warm noontide, in the twilight dusk, they strolled and played and knew each other.

And in all the world that God had created, there was no other garden like Eden, which He had made for Adam and Eve. Plants burst out of its dark earth as though to parade their petals and fronds and branches. Animals lumbered and darted and whisked and shuffled through the garden on paths that Adam had cut. The sounds of cicadas buzzing their wings, the wind pushing through high grass, the streams tumbling pell-mell over bright stones — they were all a part of Eden.

And in all the world that God had created, there was no other tree like the Tree of the Knowledge of Good and Evil. Its leaves were silver, its branches copper. When the sun sparkled through its branches and leapt off its yellow fruit, the whole tree shone. Moss hugged the base of the trunk, cool even in the heat of the day, and the tree rose out of its green sleeve as straight as if it had been ruled.

On this particular morning, Eve looked up into the tree. Its bark was too smooth to climb, and its branches usually too high to grasp. But today the fruit was so heavy, it pulled the branches down to within reach.

If she stretched, she could just circle the trunk with her arms and touch fingertips to fingertips. It was cool under the branches, and the silvery light changed the color of her hair and skin so that she, too, seemed to shine — like God, she thought. At her feet, the grass was still parted where the serpent had trailed away.

This is a new thing, she sensed, although new things were not unusual. In her long lifetime she had never awakened to a day when there had not been something new. From the day when her soul had opened and God had brought her by the hand to Adam, to this day, the garden had always shown her surprising things. Yesterday there had been the fern tendrils curling in green wheels of new growth. The day before there had been the bird that she and Adam had followed through the afternoon, a brown and red bird with a chirping song. And the day before that there had been the two turtles flopping over each other into the mud, poking their legs out to heft their shells along. And just today there had been the new lion cubs, still blind, bumbling around their mother, who looked at them with such happiness.

Eve wondered what it would be like to be a mother.

The serpent had given her more to think about, and a new thing that she was not sure she liked. It had made her feel — well, she couldn't understand what the feeling was. Eden was a place of perfect love, so she couldn't recognize the serpent's hate. It was a place of perfect safety, so she couldn't

recognize the serpent's danger. But it had made her think, for a moment, that God could say something that was not.

God was always new. She smiled when she thought of her walks with Him, just before the evening sun slept. There was never a day when He did not show her more of Himself. This was different from Adam. Him she knew like she knew herself. He was always Adam, as unchanging as the sound of the water trilling, or the feel of the pebbly shore, or the sight of the morning sun. He was always Adam.

And even though He kept showing new things to her, God was always God. But now the serpent had shown a new thing. She thought back to yesterday . . .

"You will not die," the serpent promised.

"But God has told us not to eat the fruit of this tree. If we do, we will die."

"Nothing dies here," the serpent countered. "God has told you a thing that is not."

Eve looked at the serpent, not understanding.

"If I was to tell you that the water would not quench your thirst, then I would be telling you the thing that is not."

"Yes," said Eve, nodding. "But why say such a thing?"

"Perhaps I would want to keep you from the water. Perhaps I would want it all for myself."

"But why would you want such a thing? There is more than you can drink."

"Because I would want to be greater than you. Because I could make you serve me."

Eve considered this. It was not something she had ever thought before.

Eve at the
Tree of
the
Knowledge
of Good
and Evil

—

7

"Do you see now?" asked the serpent, slowly, softly.

"No," said Eve. "If you kept me from this water, I would go somewhere else."

"But suppose there was no 'somewhere else'? Suppose this was the only stream?"

Eve looked at the nearby stream, puzzling over this. "Then, I suppose, I would die."

"Unless you took the water from me," said the serpent. "Now do you see? God has made only one tree like this. He has told you the thing that is not so that you will not eat from it. He has kept you from it so that you will serve Him, and He will have it to Himself. But listen to this: You can take it from Him. All you have to do is reach up, choose a piece of fruit, and eat it. And you will not die. You will be like Him."

Eve frowned. "Why should I want to be like God?"

It was the serpent's turn to look puzzled. Could it be that there was a creature in this universe that did not want the thing he wanted — to be like God? He remembered the time — who knows how long ago — that he had fallen away from God's throne.

Eve turned away from the silver tree; the serpent's promises about it did not interest her. She would have to think about whether God could say the thing that was not. But she knew one thing: she did not want to be like God. She wanted to be Eve. She was Eve, Adam was Adam, God was God.

"Serpent," she called back over her shoulder, "I have no need of this fruit. I am who I am. This cannot change."

"No," called the serpent. "You do not know who you are. How can you know, unless you eat of this tree and taste the fruit that makes gods?"

Eve stopped.

"Are you one of the animals you care for, merely eating and sleeping?"

The serpent wound his way closer to her. "Do you not see that you are closer to God than any of these? Why should you not change? Why should you not become as He is?"

"Because He said not to."

"Just as I might tell you not to drink from the stream."

The serpent, smiling, smoothed his way through the grasses into the higher brush.

So today Eve had come back to the tree and looked up into its branches.

Now she reached up her hand, and a cloud covered the sun and dimmed the light on the fruit. As soon as she touched it, the fruit fell from the branch into her hand. It was smooth and round and cool. The smell from it was heavy, and it seeped around her like smoke so that soon she could smell nothing else. She put the fruit to her lips; its skin was moist and swelling with all the juices inside that wanted to gush out into the world.

And then she bit. Deeply, deeply into the fruit she bit. And it was good — for a moment.

Quickly Eve finished half the fruit, its juices oozing down her chin. Then, holding the core tightly, she ran through the garden, scattering fearful animals. Her eyes darted back and forth, searching for Adam.

Genesis 2:20 – 3:7

Noah BY THE WINDOW OF THE ARK

Noah stood at the window of the Ark.

He had been standing there a very long time. His back leg, braced against the slant of the deck, was tired. His shoulders, pressed through the tiny window, ached. His eyes, unused to the brightness of the blue sky, teared. But he hardly noticed any of those things. He was watching for the white flash of feathers that would tell him that all was at an end. Or was it a beginning? He hardly knew.

Behind him the animals adjusted as best they could to the slant of the deck. For some this was no trouble at all. The monkeys seemed to actually enjoy it, scampering around the rafters and screaming out like lunatics. The dogs liked to race up the slant, their tongues hanging out of the sides of their mouths, and then race down, going so fast that they couldn't stop before crashing into the side of the Ark. But for the oxen and the horses it was a trial and a tribulation. They weren't sure if they should take the slant sideways, or head up into it, or keep their heads down; mostly they kept moving around and around. Shem — who was in charge of them — would be glad when he could get them out.

His sons had grown used to the Ark. It had taken them no time to pitch their walk to the pitch of the waters. The constant cry of the animals, their stampings and bellowings, the groaning of the timbers, the smells — Lord, the smells! — had all become familiar. Touching animals they had never touched before, placing a hand on a warthog, watching the lambings and calvings and hatchings — there had been so much to keep them busy besides the chores that they all had had little time to think.

Except Noah. Since the rain had started, he had not been able to stop thinking. He thought about the animals that had still been outside the Ark when God closed the doors. He thought about his vineyards and house, about the cities of the plains, about his neighbors, about all those whom he had never met, about the children playing in the streets who had been called in by worried mothers when the rain began to fall.

Noah had wept often.

But not since the Ark had grounded upon the mountains of Ararat.

They had all been thrown down, a jumble of dogs and people and hogs and geese, barking and hollering and squealing and squawking; the jarring had spilled slops and feed and sent clay jars rolling across the deck. Ham had been the first to pull himself free from the pile and rush to the window. But Noah had reached the window almost at the same time and had pushed his son away. He had unhooked the latches, hefted the planking, set up the prop, and looked out.

And then he had laughed.

Ham had wondered if he could have heard right. But when Noah had pulled his head back in the window, Ham had seen that his father was truly laughing.

Then Ham had looked out. What he had seen was a world as new and as fresh as if God had just now parted the waters and sent them to their places. The mountains had already begun to put on their fuzz of green, but water had still flooded the valleys. No place to plant there, or even build yet. But Ham had seen land where before there had been only water, and the damp, musty, earthy smells of land had reached up to him.

Then the long waiting had begun, and it had seemed longer than when they had floated above the mountains and had looked out on nothing but water. Every day, sometime between the haying and the watering and the mucking out, each of them had stolen to the window to watch as the green spread lower on the mountains and the water soaked away in the valleys. And finally, one day, when Noah had looked out on the dawn, there had been no more water to reflect the sun.

Then had come the trials. First was the raven that Noah had sent cawing, cawing, cawing down the valley. All day — as now — Noah had stood, back leg braced against the slant of the deck, at the window. By nightfall, the raven hadn't come back. It had brought no sign.

That had been a bad night for them all. No one had spoken. Even the animals had seemed discouraged.

They had waited a long time before the next trial, hoping that the green that was now fully in the valleys would mean the land was dry. Then Noah had sent out a dove, and again had waited all day for it to bring some sign.

Unlike the raven, the dove had come back at nightfall. But it had brought no sign.

No one had said anything. What was there to say? They had gone about the chores as though they would be doing them forever. Suddenly the Ark had seemed like a prison.

They had waited a long time again, almost afraid to send out another bird. Until finally, this morning, without a word to anyone, Noah had taken the dove once more from its roost and set it on the windowsill. It had flown away, eagerly stretching its wings against the cool breezes that blew up the sides of the mountains. The breezes had lofted the bird into the sky and then guided it in a quick flurry of wings down, down to the green valley below the Ark. Noah had braced his back leg, and waited.

He had been standing there for a very long time.

He did not know his wife was watching him, wondering how he would take this next disappointment. He did not know that she took up the chores he was ignoring, that she murmured her prayers, looking anxiously at him, worried more for Noah than for all the animals that they cared for. Watching his back and the patterns of light that flickered across him from the nearby candles, she felt such a long, old love within her that she wanted to run up the deck and embrace him. But he did not even know that. She slipped a troublesome strand of hair beneath her kerchief and went to help her daughters-in-law gather eggs.

If she had watched a moment longer, she would have seen Noah's ancient back suddenly straighten. She would have seen him lean further out the window. And then out even further, almost as though he were trying to escape the Ark. And then she would have seen him shoulder his way back in, holding in his hand the white dove, holding it so tenderly that it might have been the greatest treasure in the world.

As it was, she turned when her daughters-in-law gasped in unison. Noah stood before her with love in his eyes, the love of troubles borne together for a

lifetime. On his shoulder roosted the dove, already fast asleep, her head under her wing. In his hand was a fresh olive leaf no bigger than a dove could carry.

Smiling, Noah reached over and gently untied his wife's kerchief, then slid the leaf of promise into her hair.

Genesis 6:1–8:22

Hagar,
THE EGYPTIAN MAIDSERVANT

The words thudded into Hagar's heart like a dull tent peg into hardened sand.

"Sarah is with child."

Impossible. It could not be true. Abraham was a hundred years old already. Sarah was well past the age of childbearing. It could not be true.

But again and again that hot dusty morning she heard the news until even her son, Ishmael, came running into the tent, giggling with the joke of it. Sarah would have a child, he said. Can you imagine? Sarah with child.

After he left, the goatskin flap still shaking in the hot breeze, Hagar held her robes around her face and wept bitter tears. And no one tried to comfort her. Not Abraham — he was too busy preparing the celebration. Not her maidservants — they knew how Sarah would react to the favorites of Hagar.

Not Ishmael — he didn't know what the birth of this child would mean for him. The hope and joy of fourteen years, gone in a moment.

"Sarah is with child."

Hagar rose and tied the tent flaps. It seemed that she was moving in her memories so that when her hands reached out to secure the ties, she could not tell whether it was in the past or the present, whether the sobbing that she heard was that of fourteen years ago or now. Perhaps it was both.

Before Ishmael had been born — Ishmael, the most precious gift that God had blessed her with — she had been nothing but a maidservant herself, bought by the wealthy Abraham from a caravan out of Egypt. She had learned quickly how to please her mistress, Sarah, who was not an easy woman to please. She had learned Sarah's moods, and she knew when to leave Sarah alone and when to comfort or amuse her. She had learned what Sarah's favorite foods were, and she fixed them in surprising ways that delighted her mistress. She had learned the songs that Sarah loved, and she had learned to sing them so that they would soothe Sarah into sleep.

So no one in the camp had been surprised when it was Hagar whom Sarah chose to bear a child for Abraham. It was Hagar who would birth the son that would not fill Sarah's dry womb. Hagar, the Egyptian maidservant, would bear the son of Abraham.

But once Hagar had become pregnant, she had begun to taunt Sarah. She would remind Sarah of what she did not have in a hundred small ways. She would lean close to Abraham and laugh and smile when he inquired after her health. She would often rest her hands on her growing belly and talk to the child inside (knowing that Sarah was listening). She would point out the herds of sheep that whitened the hills and promise the child that, someday, all would be his. And she would tell the servants looking after her (loudly, so that Sarah could hear) that she knew her child — Abraham's son, her son — would look like his father.

And it was this that had become to Sarah as bitter as the waters of the sea: the child would be Hagar's son, not Sarah's. And Sarah had finally risen up in her anger and shown herself to be stronger than Hagar had expected. She had gone to Abraham. She had told him of the slights. He had nodded — she was to do as she pleased with the Egyptian maidservant. And what Sarah had pleased to do was to torment Hagar, to treat her so badly that Hagar had finally fled from the camp. She had gone out into the desert, heavy with Abraham's child, to die. She would not live to bear Abraham's heir, she had thought bitterly as she waited for heat and thirst to claim her. She would add the particles of her whitened bones to the infinite sea of sand that heaved and swirled around her.

And it was there that she had received the blessing.

She had not expected it. Certainly she had never expected it from the God of Abraham.

Out in the desert she had stopped by a spring of water, and the Lord had spoken to her. She had heard God.

"Hagar." The voice had been as gentle as crushed oil on the skin. "Hagar, return to Sarah and submit to her. I will bless you. Your descendants will be so many that you will not be able to count them. I will watch over Ishmael."

So she had returned to the camp and learned to please Sarah again.

And in the end it had all come about as she had hoped. A son was born, a beautiful son whose dark hair and eyes were his mother's, but whose strong forearms and muscled neck were his father's. Ishmael, the son of Abraham. Ishmael, the heir of Abraham. Ishmael, the son of Hagar.

But now, fourteen years later, God's words were bitter ones. Ishmael would no longer be Abraham's heir. There would be no descendants. There would be nothing.

The months passed quickly by. In some ways nothing changed. There was still the lambing to be done in the spring, the cooking to be done, the taking down and putting up of tents as the camp moved to fresh pastures.

But everything had changed. Sarah looked at Hagar now with new eyes that were deep and still. Abraham spent much of his time watching Sarah grow big with his new heir. He had never been gentle with her, but now there was nothing she wanted that he did not see to. Sarah had banned Ishmael from her tent — the boy didn't understand why, and Hagar had told him the child within Sarah tired her so that she needed quiet.

The day came, as Hagar had known it must. She had hoped that perhaps God would be good and Sarah would bear a girl-child, but she had known all along that it would be a son. And it was. Isaac. When she heard the news, Hagar went into her tent, and no one disturbed her.

During the next several days, Hagar could hear the maidservants talk as they carried water past her tent. (Did they mean for her to hear?) The baby had already opened his eyes and laughed. He had already grabbed onto his father's rough hand and sucked at his fingers. His cry was the bellow of a desert shepherd.

This talk went on week after week, and it seemed to Hagar that she overheard all of it.

After Isaac was weaned, Abraham called for all the camp to come to a great celebration. Hagar could not stay away. She dressed in her finest clothes, layer upon layer of rich damask and linen. She oiled her skin until it shone and placed a turquoise ring on her finger. Then she took Ishmael by the hand and, looking straight ahead, went to Abraham's celebration. She pretended not to notice when others moved aside to let her pass, or when Sarah turned her back to her. The rich smell of the roasting lamb, the sound of flutes and pipes, the laughter of the men gathered, the young girl holding the baby — it all seemed to be nothing to the proud face of Hagar.

And there was Abraham. Surely he . . . But he too was moving away, as though she was nothing but a slave bought out of Egypt.

But she was not just a slave. She gripped Ishmael's hand and said to him in a loud voice, so that all could hear — even Abraham and Sarah — "The new baby is your brother. Go to him." The crowd stilled, waiting to see what Ishmael would do.

But Ishmael sensed nothing of what his mother felt. He went to the baby and laughed as he picked up Isaac. He tickled Isaac under his chin until he giggled, and the laughter of Ishmael and the laughter of Isaac twined. And then the baby, holding tightly to the thumb of his brother, closed his eyes and fell asleep.

But Sarah would not have it so. She made a show of taking Isaac away from Ishmael; Isaac immediately woke and began to scream. As Sarah wrapped up her baby tightly, she looked at Ishmael, and then at Hagar. And then Hagar knew what lay beneath the deep, still darkness of Sarah's eyes.

The next day, Abraham was at her tent. He did not look at her as he told her she must go. He stretched his hand to the wilderness beyond the camp, back toward Egypt. He handed her a bundle of bread and a skin filled with water. God would be with her, he promised, because Ishmael was his son. Hagar did not answer. She took the bread and the water, called Ishmael to her side, and, without getting anything else, walked away from Abraham. She would never see him again.

So this was how Abraham's God kept his promises. The sand and rocks of the desert were his blessing. The scorpions were the descendants he spoke of. But she would not weep. She would not weep.

For three days they walked, until they could walk no more. They saw no one. Their bread was gone. Their water was gone. And Ishmael was feverish with thirst. As the morning of the fourth day dawned and the sun burned against the rocks, Hagar gathered her child in her arms and laid him in the shadow of a bush that already seemed to burn with the morning light. Then she lay down — she would not weep. Perhaps this God of Abraham's would at least be merciful enough to let her die before Ishmael.

But if Hagar would not cry, Ishmael would — long wails of terror and pain, choked with the dust in his throat. Hagar held her hands to her ears against the sound, and when it stopped, she was sure that he had died.

But he had not.

"Hagar." The voice came again as it had fourteen years ago.

"Hagar. Do not be afraid. I have heard the voice of your son. Lift him up and hold him close to you."

Hagar got quickly to her feet and clasped her son to her breast. To her surprise, his skin was cool, and he was sleeping peacefully.

"I will bless you, and make your son a great nation," the voice said. "And your descendants will be so many that you will not be able to count them."

From the place where Ishmael had lain, a spring bubbled up. Hagar looked with disbelieving eyes at the clean, cool water running into the sand with merry life. Then she wept, and not from sorrow.

Hagar woke her son. She filled the skin with water and gave him a drink. When they both had satisfied their thirst, Ishmael filled the skin again. Then, together, they rose, and Hagar looked off into the hazed distance. They had a long way to go. There was a new nation in front of them.

The Lord had told them so.

Genesis 16:1-16
18:1-15
21:1-21

THE SERVANTS OF Abraham and Isaac AT MORIAH

The strangeness of it was past all reckoning. And these two servants were used to strange ways from their master. Hadn't they followed him from Ur of the Chaldees to Haran, where they had buried Terah, Abraham's father and their old master? And then from there to Shechem and then to Bethel and down to the Negev and into Egypt. And then, after returning to Bethel (where there had been that unpleasantness with Lot's herdsmen), on to Hebron, then back to the Negev and the country of King Abimelech. They had traveled far and wide, all over Canaan, at the word of Abraham's God. And how often that word had been so strange.

But these servants never complained. They had been with Abraham's family since before he was born. So when he had woken them while the stars were still bright and only he awake in camp, they had risen. And when he had asked them to fetch a donkey, they had fetched it and loaded it with supplies for a day's travel. And when they had set off — the two servants, Abraham, and his son Isaac — they had not asked where they were going. They knew all the signs: it was Abraham's God sending him somewhere new.

The boy Isaac was excited by the strangeness of the early morning. He had probably never seen the camp so quiet and still before. And he was its joy. Everyone in Abraham's camp had laughed and wept when a son had been born to Abraham. That had been a special night in camp, and there was not a one among them all who did not bless Abraham's God for what He had sent as a blessing to them. The two servants remembered the timbrels, the dancers whirling with their high calls against the firelight, the horns poking toward the stars, and the chinging, chinging bells singing in the night air. That had been a special night in camp, and there was not a one among them all who did not bless Abraham's God for what he had sent as a blessing to them.

The cold of the purple morning sky tipped the servants' fingers, so when the sun rose, they lifted their faces to it; they felt its light in their bones, which were still stiff from a chilled night. Isaac ran ahead, found something shiny along the path, put it into a pouch strapped to his side, and ran on again. The cold of the dawn, the heat of the mid-morning, the cool of the evening — all were one to him.

Under a stand of tamarack trees they ate their noon meal, Isaac still running about, playing with the donkey, shimmying up the trees. Abraham ate slowly, as if the dates and honeycakes were dust in his mouth. He did not speak with the two servants who sat by him in the shade, seeking shelter from the noon sun.

"Father." It was Isaac, calling from a branch that stretched above, his feet dangling toward them. "Where are we going?"

"To Moriah." That was all.

"And why to Moriah?"

"To sacrifice to God."

The
Servants
of
Abraham
and
Isaac
at
Moriah

—

23

"But we haven't brought anything to make the sacrifice. We have only the embers."

"Just so," he said. "We must gather the wood now." Abraham motioned to the two servants, and they rose and began collecting branches that had fallen from the tamarack trees. Isaac climbed down to help. They bundled the branches together and tied them to the back of the donkey that brayed and kicked out at the load. Isaac laughed at the donkey's stuck-out teeth, then smoothed his hand along its muzzle to calm it.

"Moriah is not far off," he soothed. Then he himself took the reins and led the donkey out onto the road.

By late afternoon the sun had heated the air so that it shimmered ahead of them, and the servants remembered another time when Abraham had told them of the air shimmering and three strangers coming out of it to announce the birth of Isaac. Now Abraham was as silent as the stones they passed, and he seemed not to let himself look at the boy. When the servants glanced at him out of the corners of their eyes, it seemed that he was crying, but it may have simply been the sweat that ran down all of their faces. They walked on in the heat and the dust; even Isaac had stopped running now.

The sun was already starting to go down when they reached the foot of the mountain, and the red of the sky and the red of the land blended together so that you couldn't tell where the one left off and the other started. They all stopped at the foot of the sharp ascent, and the donkey looked up to the heights and brayed loudly. The sound woke Abraham from his silence.

"Stay here with the donkey," he instructed the servants. It was all he needed to say; these servants were used to his quick, sharp commands. But on this day, Abraham hesitated, then went on as though he needed to explain — or perhaps because he did not want to take the first steps toward what lay ahead for him on the mountain.

"The boy and I will go on up the mountain." A long pause. "We will

worship there." Another long pause. "And then we will both come back to you." It seemed that Abraham said this quickly and with a rush of tears, though in the fading light the servants could not be sure. It was all very strange.

The servants unloaded the wood from the donkey; Abraham took it and strapped it to Isaac's back. Isaac looked around as if something were missing. "Father," he said, "we have the wood and the fire" — he glanced at the pot of embers Abraham was holding — "but where is the lamb for our burnt offering?"

"God will provide the lamb, my son." Abraham's voice was unsteady, but his answer seemed enough for Isaac; he turned and started up the path. After a glance back at the servants, Abraham followed his son. But that glance was enough to tell the servants that what lay up on that mountain for Abraham would take away his heart's desire.

Once Abraham and Isaac were out of sight, the two servants unloaded the donkey; it would be a long journey back if they were to begin it tonight. They did not speak of Abraham; it would have been unseemly for servants to question their master. They wiped the sweat off the donkey and threw a blanket over his back so that he would not take a chill in the cooling night air. Then they fed him wheat grain and gave him water by pouring some from a waterskin into a hollow stone. They themselves each ate from a loaf of barley bread and drank from the waterskin; then they sat down to wait.

They did not wait very long.

Before it was fully dark, the mountain of Moriah rumbled with the presence of Abraham's God. They felt the shaking deep in their bones, and they hid their eyes from the mountain. They had long ago heard that Abraham's God was not to be seen. The rumbling grew louder, and louder, and louder, like thunder beneath the ground, like the skin drums that had boomed, boomed, boomed through the night at Isaac's birth. And then, when it seemed as if the rumbling would rip the mountain apart, there came a white light like all the stars merged into one, and a single word, called out in triumph and fear through the whole world: "Abraham!"

The rumbling stopped. The servants kept their eyes on the ground and would not look up.

At dawn, Abraham and Isaac returned. Abraham came down the trail first, his faced smeared by smoke yet full of light. He walked as though everything he had ever wanted had been given to him. Isaac walked behind, and he walked slowly and thoughtfully. Fresh bloodstains were smeared across both of their cloaks, and there was blood on their hands.

Nothing was said. The servants loaded the donkey and followed Abraham, who led them down the trail. Behind followed Isaac, his arms crossed over his chest, his hands clutching his shoulders.

The strangeness of it was past all reckoning.

*Genesis 21:1-7
22:1-19*

Jacob, THE SONS OF LEAH, AND THE SONS OF RACHEL

God of my father Isaac, is what I hear possible?"

"It is," said Reuben. "It is all true. Joseph is alive. He is a great man. A ruler in Egypt. He has sent us back here with wagons from Pharaoh himself to carry us all back to the land of Goshen. It is a land of plenty, Father, a land where our sheep can graze, and where we will never be hungry again."

But Jacob was not interested in the land.

"How can this be?" he asked, spreading his arms wide and looking at his sons through misted eyes. "How can this be? You yourselves brought me his coat. You saw how it was torn and bloodied. I keep it here. I can show you now."

Reuben shook his head. "No, Father, Joseph is alive. He is in Egypt, and he sends for you."

Tears filled the deep lines that the sun had etched into Jacob's face. The hands that at one time could pick up two sheep at a time quivered, and the shoulders that had once heaved rocks to build wells and swung staffs to fend off jackals sagged with age.

"How can this be?" he repeated.

Beside Jacob stood Benjamin, whom Jacob loved more than all of his other sons. He loved him as much for himself as for his lost brother Joseph. Reuben, looking at Benjamin now, could not help but see how much he looked like Joseph. And he could not help but feel the old jealousy rise again. But he held it down. The time was past for such things. God had done something extraordinary.

"Father," said Reuben, "there is much I have to tell you, and little time. We must prepare to go to Egypt."

But Jacob suddenly grabbed Benjamin and drew him close. "We will not go down to Egypt until I know that what you say is true."

"Father," Reuben insisted, "it is true. Benjamin himself can tell you."

But Jacob merely stared back at Reuben and his other sons, holding tightly to Benjamin, and Reuben knew that his father would not leave his land unless he understood how it could be that Joseph was still alive. Reuben sat down, crossed his legs, and sighed. "Then, Father," he said, "I shall tell you how it is true."

"Father, the coat that I took from Joseph was his, but I took it from him when he was still alive." Jacob's eyes opened wide. He breathed quickly, listening to every word as if it was the words themselves that gave him his life.

"You must have known that we were jealous of him, Father. You must have known. A hundred times a day you showed us that he was the favored one. He was always the one to receive the best of the lambs, the best of the

Jacob,
the Sons
of Leah,
and the
Sons of
Rachel

—

29

pastures, the new coat. He was the one who sat by your right hand and drank from your cup. How could we not resent him and the love that you showed him?"

"But you were *all* my sons," said Jacob.

"No," Reuben shook his head sadly, tears in his eyes now. "We were not. Not like Joseph. And not" — he said, pointing — "not like Benjamin. We have never been like the sons of Rachel to you."

Jacob said nothing. He knew that it was true. And he could not help it.

"So," Reuben continued, "we did something terrible. Something terrible against God and you and Joseph. When Joseph came to find us one day at Dothan, we took his fine new coat, bound him, and threw him into an empty cistern. We wanted to kill him, but God had something else planned. We sold him to a caravan of Ishmaelites heading to trade in Egypt. Then we slaughtered a goat, tore the coat, dipped it in the goat's blood, and brought it back to you."

Jacob bowed his head to the ground. He could hardly understand everything that was stirring in him. Could Joseph actually be alive? He felt a place in his heart warm where for years there had been only terrible cold. To see Joseph again — walking, talking, laughing, instead of only moving through his dreams! But intermingled with the beginning of joy was the deep sorrow over what his sons had done — and the part he had played in it. Reuben was right. He was right.

"And when we came back with the bloodied coat, we thought you would turn to us, your other sons who loved you. But you did not."

"No," Jacob agreed, "I did not."

There was silence in the tent of Jacob, the silence of all those years of love spilt into the sand — for nothing.

"Go on," said Jacob finally, sadly.

"All these years," Reuben continued, "we thought he was dead, or a slave at best, which is like being dead. We never thought we would see him again. And then, when we did, we did not recognize him."

"You saw him?"

"Yes."

"You were sure it was he?"

"We were sure. He asked for you by name. He cried over Benjamin as only a brother can cry. He knew us all."

"And he took no vengeance upon you."

"None. He said that everything that had happened had been God's plan. It was God who brought him to Egypt — to save that land and to save us."

"But he was sold as a slave. How could a slave rise to such power?"

Reuben shook his head in wonder. "Only God," was all he said.

Jacob rose to his feet, unaided. Usually he leaned upon Benjamin to walk. But now he strode to the tent flap and flung it aside. Outside was a line of wagons decorated with the flat gold and black of Egypt; the wagons were tethered to fine horses. Behind them stretched twenty mules burdened with gifts of grain and other provisions. Jacob turned back inside the tent, the sun from outside shining behind him. "How can this be?" he said again, not to Reuben but to himself. He let the tent flap droop in the heat and came and settled himself on the rugs that softened the tent floor. He heaved one of the goatskin flasks to his lips and drank the date wine, trying to clear his head.

"Tell me of your meeting with him."

"There has been more than one," explained Reuben. "Last year, when we went down to Egypt, we met him for the first time. He knew us, but we didn't know who he was. He had changed more than we have. He was dressed in all the splendor of the Egyptians; we were in goatskins." Bitterly,

Reuben wondered if Jacob would have been pleased, but again he held his anger down. "He accused us of being spies and sent us home, keeping Simeon as hostage."

"This I remember," said Jacob.

"And do you remember that he told us that Simeon would be held until we brought Benjamin back with us to Egypt to prove we were telling the truth?"

"Yes," sighed Jacob, sadly and quietly.

"But you would not send Benjamin."

Silence fell like blocks of rock between them. Outside the horses were snorting in the breeze.

"Go on." The regret hung heavy in Jacob's voice.

"Only when we were all starving would you send Benjamin, and so we went back and met with Joseph again, but still we did not know him. He brought us to his house, filled our sacks with grain, feasted us all as if we were celebrating, and then sent us on our way."

"Then how did you learn that this was Joseph?"

"Because he is as cunning as a man who steals his brother's blessing. He hid a silver cup in the grain that Benjamin's donkey carried, then sent his soldiers after us to discover it. The soldiers brought us back to Egypt, back to Joseph, and he said that because of the theft, he would make a slave of Benjamin. We thought that what we had done to Joseph had come back on our own heads."

"That is the way of God," said Jacob. "What we do comes back to us, good or ill. It is what my grandfather Abraham discovered, and what Isaac discovered after him."

"And now we have discovered it too," whispered Reuben. "Joseph held out his hand over us, and when we thought he would imprison us all, the tears broke from his eyes and he cried, 'I am Joseph! Is my father still living?' We could not answer him, we were so stunned."

"And afraid," added Jacob.

"And afraid," agreed Reuben.

"And sorry to see your brother alive again."

"No, not sorry." Saying it, Reuben realized it was true. "Not now. Not when we see the hand of God in him."

"It is a fearful thing, to see the hand of God in a man," said Jacob, speaking as though he were remembering things from long ago. He stood. At his right side was Benjamin, the son of Rachel. And in front of him were the sons of Leah, his first wife. The blessing that Abraham had carried had gone to Joseph; God had seen to that. But it was up to Jacob now to pass on another blessing to these sons of his.

He went to a woven basket in the corner of the tent and pulled from it a beautiful but torn coat, stained with blood, carefully folded. He took it outside, his sons following. Then he threw it into the cooking fire that burned redly in the late afternoon sun. The coat blackened, caught fire, and was gone, the smoke rising to heaven.

Then Jacob turned to the sons of Leah with tears in his eyes.

Genesis 37:2-4, 12-35
42:1-45:28

Pharaoh's Daughter
AND THE ARK IN THE NILE

Pharaoh's daughter was bored. She sat by the window of her rooms, looking down into the courtyard where the children of her servant women played among the palms. They ran wobbly-kneed after each other, shrieking. One tossed a golden ball back and forth with her mother, while another sat cuddled with his mother in a hammock, falling into sleep as she stroked his hair. Pharaoh's daughter turned away.

She dismissed the servant waving a fan of peacock feathers over her. Immediately the air stilled and the heat settled in. She played with the rings on her fingers, watching the jewels catch the light. She took off her thick wig, threaded through with silver, and left it on the window ledge. Her hands found the necklace of golden bees that circled her throat, and she played with them, her blank eyes looking across the room. She was bored.

She stood up from her chair by the window. She felt an urge to see her father, but she could not go to him unless he called for her. He had not done this in many days, and she worried that she had somehow displeased him. Though her servants told her that Pharaoh was terribly busy with a problem about the Hebrew slaves, she still felt that something had been lost between them, and she did not know how to get it back.

She decided to bathe.

Two claps of her hands brought six servants, as though they were waiting just beyond the shimmering curtains to her apartment. They clothed her in a *shenti* of white linen, the edges of the long robe tasseled with gold. One old servant, clicking her tongue, fetched the heavy wig and readjusted it upon her head. Another fit a gold circlet over her forehead, while another adjusted a flat collar of layered blue enamel that covered her neck. She let them re-paint the black around her eyes and lengthen her eyebrows with the dark, inky colors in the little pots they brought. Through all this she said nothing. Her servants worked on her as though she was a doll.

But finally she grew impatient with their attentions. "Enough," she said sharply, standing up. The loose linen flowing around her, she crossed the parquet floor, the servants following her like the wake following her barge on the Nile. The happy shrieks of the children faded behind her.

She walked down the crushed stone path to the river as though she were part of a ceremony. Her eyes looked straight ahead, and she did not see — or would not allow herself to see — the bowing servants and the lower court officials she passed. They were nothing to her at all, no more than the birds that flew across her line of sight. They were simply part of the landscape, and it all bored her.

But the Nile never bored her. It was always different, even though she always came to the same place to bathe. Sometimes the water would be churned up, white and frothy, from some storm upriver. Sometimes the water would be brown and low, and it would lie still and thirsty. Sometimes it would be clear and bubbly, especially after the spring rains had passed. It was as important to her, she thought, as her own blood, and somehow that idea sent a shiver up her back. She tightened the *shenti* around herself.

Her servants, used to her moods, followed her quietly and hoped that the water would save some part of this day. And it did. The water was clear, the current sure but not too strong, the feel of it cool but not cold. The sunlight skipped across its surface, and when Pharaoh's daughter parted the reeds at the river's edge and stepped in, giggling like a young girl, the servants knew that something had changed in her.

She waded in deeper, up to her waist, exclaiming and splashing and laughing with pleasure. Soon her wig hung heavy with water, and the ink around her eyes ran. She splashed water back at her servants, calling playfully to them. Probably it was those calls that woke the child in the reeds.

Pharaoh's daughter heard it first — the thin, small call of a tiny baby, too young to know what it wants, too young to wait for whatever it is. She could not tell where the sound was coming from, since it seemed to be from across the water, and that could not be. But indeed it was. She pushed into the thick papyrus reeds — the same ones that her servants gathered for her sailmaker to make the finest sails in all Egypt — following the cries.

"Lady," called one of her servants.

"Wait there," she said sharply. And then she saw the little ark tied securely to the reeds. She gestured with one ring-laden hand, and one of the servants waded into the river, untied the basket, and brought it to her mistress. With a quick nod, Pharaoh's daughter dismissed the servant. She wanted to be alone with her discovery.

The ark was not beautiful, especially to one who never saw anything ugly.

It had obviously been woven together hurriedly. But it was tight; no water had leaked in. She took the cover off, laid it in the water, and picked up the child that now looked at her with wide-open eyes, trying to focus. Well, the baby was wet, thought the princess, but not from the Nile. The baby reached toward her, and she smiled.

Pharaoh's daughter put her nose to the baby's and rubbed it back and forth. The child squealed with laughter and grabbed the golden bees that circled her neck. She let him play with them, then took the necklace off and let him put one in his mouth. He didn't like the taste and spat it out. When he screwed up his face to cry again, she rocked him up and down, then dabbled his feet in the water, then tickled his face with a reed.

"Lady!" It was one of her boldest servants who called.

"I'm coming," she called back, and the servants looked at each other in wonder. When Pharaoh's daughter came out from the cocoon of reeds, she carried a bundle of baby. "Come see what I have," she called gaily, hardly able to get the words out through her laughter.

The servants waded up to her, crowding around, pulling aside the cloth blanket that swaddled the child.

"A baby."

"A little boy."

"In the reeds?"

And then one of the servants said the word that chilled the sun and stilled their laughter. "A Hebrew child."

At the word, Pharaoh's daughter hugged the baby closely to her and covered his face with the blanket. "The gods have sent me this child on the back of the Nile."

"But Pharaoh has ordered that all the male children of the Hebrews are to be . . ."

"Silence! I have told you that the child is a gift from the gods."

In the heavy silence that fell, a sudden shriek from the baby cut through the air. Pharaoh's daughter jiggled him up and down, up and down, but the child kept crying. She brought him up onto the banks of the river and swung him through the air, and still he kept crying.

"He is hungry," suggested one of the servants.

"Yes," Pharaoh's daughter answered simply, and she did not know what to do. But when she looked to the river, the answer came.

A young girl was climbing up onto the riverbank, a reed stuck in her hair. She wore a shawl made from the same material as the blanket that covered the baby, and her eyes and forehead showed what the baby would look like in years to come. "Princess," she asked, as though she had been listening, "shall I find one of the Hebrew women to nurse the child for you?"

The princess smiled at this new gift from the sacred river. "What is your name?"

"Miriam."

"Then Miriam, go find me a Hebrew woman to nurse this child. Tell her that the child is safe, and that when he is weaned, she will bring him to the palace, and he will be the son of the daughter of Pharaoh, and his name will be Moses, because I drew him out of the water."

The girl ran off, her robe dripping water down her bare legs. Pharaoh's daughter turned back toward the apartments, holding the baby that was still crying. "Hush, little one, hush," she cooed. Pharaoh's daughter was no longer bored.

Exodus 1:22
2:1-10

Moses AT THE RED SEA

Pharaoh caught them hemmed in by the desert, pressed back against the Red Sea, not far from Pi Hahiroth. Standing in his chariot on a rocky crest above them, he smiled grimly to himself. He had gone into battles against Amorites and Ethiopians and Sumerians where everything counted on his maneuvering for position. But here there was no need to maneuver. All the advantages were on his side. He could plunge straight on, or send part of his army to attack from the north. In fact, he thought, watching the Hebrew camp below, he could possibly send another part of his army to attack from the south. Usually it was not a good tactic to divide an army into three units, but with the speed he could get from his chariots, it might be worth risking such a division.

Night was falling now, and the wind was coming up. He would wait. He would let the panic that the sight of his army set off among the slaves below grow during the night, until the Hebrews might themselves turn against

Moses and Aaron and hand them over. Pharaoh would bring those two back to Egypt in chains. Perhaps he would blind them first. He would take vengeance on the Hebrews for all the firstborn sons who had died at the hand of their God. And he would bring the rest back as slaves — again. His smile grew broader.

While Pharaoh watched the Hebrew camp, his servants — who knew his moods and had guessed his strategy — set up his tent. It was hard work, since the wind was rising off the water, but they managed to peg the tent into the sand and make it ready for Pharaoh. Inside, two servants spread rich carpets and hung lamps and tinkling chimes. Another used cloves to cleanse the water in leather flasks. A priest now stood by, ready with incense.

Outside, a silent signal from Pharaoh set the camp against the darkness left by the sinking of Ra over the western horizon. Guards were posted, and sentries sent to the north and south along the Red Sea coast to ensure that the Hebrews could not steal away silently during the night. There was little chance that the Hebrews could move, especially with all the women and children and slow oxen they had with them, but Pharaoh would not be humiliated again. He directed the soldiers to build extra fires to show the size of his huge army. (This would make the panic among the Hebrews grow.) And he had all his banners set high on the crest so that they would show at first light.

Pharaoh had hoped to pick out Moses from the crowds on the beach, but the darkness had gathered and the wind had grown wild, sucking up a whirlwind of sand and spinning it in place just between the two armies. The whirlwind glowed strangely on the eastern side, throwing a soft light on the Hebrews. It made Pharaoh feel uneasy, this odd cloud. He wanted nothing to interrupt what he would do come dawn. He retired to his tent and complained about the water.

The wind blew strongly all night long. It frightened the tethered horses, who pawed at the ground and hid behind each other to try to escape the sand that pelleted their bodies. The soldiers cloaked themselves and gathered around the fires that sputtered in the gusts. No matter how they set their backs against the wind, it seemed to whirl around and sting the sand into their faces. Tents blew down across the camp, and in that wind they could not be set up again. Pharaoh's servants counted themselves lucky that his tent held.

It was a long night for the Egyptians. Their only comfort was in knowing that the wind was probably even more terrible close to the water, where the Hebrews were camped.

Before dawn the wind died down and Pharaoh came out of his tent. He was dressed magnificently. Gold wreathed his neck, and his armbands flashed with the red and blue of rubies and sapphires. A purple cloak hung to the armored greaves around his shins, and in his right hand was the spear that Ramses had used to conquer almost all the world. His soldiers could see it in his face: Today would be a day of blood.

But sudden cries from his sentries told Pharaoh that not everything would be as he had imagined. He strode through the camp, soldiers scattering out of his way, and when he reached the crest over the Hebrew camp, he looked down and saw . . . nothing.

Well, not exactly nothing. There were the remains of a camp hastily abandoned — some wagons, a tent flapping easily in the breeze, fires still smoldering, empty wineskins. The Hebrews were gone.

But it was not hard to see where they had gone. Leading straight out from the camp, leading as straight as a spear, was a path across the sea so wide that twenty — no, twenty-five — chariots could ride side by side along it. On either side the waters stood bunched up, pushed there by the night's gusts, bristling with foam at the top and heaving against the wind. And far, far away, so far that he could not be sure what he saw, Pharaoh could just make out the

Hebrews, fleeing on ground as dry as that which he stood upon now.

For a moment Pharaoh hesitated. He had seen the power of this God before, though he had been skeptical of it at first. He remembered the first great plague — the blood that had filled the Nile and sent the fish rotting and stinking to the shores. But the magicians of the land could work that same dark art, so Pharaoh had remained unmoved. But then there had been the locusts, the black cloud of locusts that had covered his fields and destroyed his harvest. And there had been the three days of darkness over Egypt when the air had been so thick that he could not breathe. None of the magicians could do these things. And deep in his heart, Pharaoh was sure that the gods of Egypt could not do these things.

But he was Pharaoh. He felt the eyes of his army upon him. Already he had given in to the Hebrews, letting them loot the temples and leave Egypt with the wealth that he had gathered through conquest. He had let the Hebrew slaves make demands of him. And his people had seen him give in.

Not now. Not again.

He set his face, grim and hard, and signaled for his chariot. "This will be short work," he called out loudly so that all would hear him and know that he, Pharaoh, was not afraid to ride down to the bed of the sea and destroy the Hebrews.

When his horses thudded up through the sand, pulling his painted chariot behind them, he stepped in and pointed with his spear down to the remains of the Hebrew camp. His driver slapped the reins across the sweating horses, holding them against the panic in their rolling eyes. Moving quickly, Pharaoh's army organized itself behind him, rank upon rank of chariots with spiked wheels and armored horses, and followed him from the crest of the desert down to the sea. The front ranks held the archers who would thin out the scattering Hebrews as the army got nearer to them. The rest were lancers with long iron spears who knew their work well.

At the edge of the path that led into the sea, Pharaoh paused again, his arm raised to stop the army. Everything was still. The only sound was the foaming of the waves seventy feet above them on either side. His soldiers expected a speech, he knew. But Pharaoh felt sick. Is this fear? he wondered. Or is it something else?

He turned to his army, men who had fought for him, for Egypt, in a dozen battles. They all knew what he knew: There would be no danger from the Hebrews. They were slaves who would be easily destroyed. But Pharaoh suddenly wondered if his men knew this other thing: That the Hebrew God was strong.

"What we do now," he shouted, "we do for the honor of the gods of Egypt. They give us the victory. They show that they are stronger than the God of Egypt's slaves." A cheer went up from the army. Pharaoh turned back and looked again at the brimming waves on either side. He hoped wildly that the gods of Egypt were more than the stone he sometimes thought they were. Then he motioned the army ahead. Within minutes the entire Egyptian army was within the valley of waters held back by the wind.

The ground was hard, packed by the feet of the Hebrews that had passed over it the night before. Pharaoh would not let himself look to either side, though he could sense his driver peering back and forth. His horses, their ears pulled straight back, panted heavily, white sweat lathering down their sides. Pharaoh commanded the driver to move faster, and beneath him he felt the rumble of his army that shook the earth. The shaking ground made him feel strong.

As the sky grew lighter and lighter, the Egyptians drew closer and closer to the Hebrew army, which was just climbing out of the path and onto the shore. Pharaoh urged his driver to move even faster; he could see Moses, and he wanted to be the one to capture and humble his enemy. The earthshaking rumble of his army grew louder and louder as the chariots rushed toward the

kill, and Pharaoh laughed at the speed and the wind and the rumbling and the sight of the Hebrew stragglers panicking away from his chariots.

And then, suddenly, the rumbling stopped and Pharaoh lurched forward in his chariot, almost thrown out. Horses crashed into each other behind him, and their screaming as the spiked wheels of the chariots sliced into their legs was horrible. Everything, he saw, had changed in an instant. Mud everywhere, and his chariots up to their hubcaps in it. His men whipping at the straining horses. The neat ranks of chariots broken into confusion. The gleaming armor of his men covered in mud.

"Leave the chariots!" he shouted above the screaming. "Leave them and follow me!"

Enraged, Pharaoh held up his spear and looked toward the shore. There stood Moses, spreading his arms wide, holding his staff out over the path. Pharaoh lowered his spear. He heard the sound of the foaming waves change, felt a new wind on his face. And then he knew that the gods of Egypt were only stone after all.

Exodus 13:17–14:31

Deborah and Barak

In the hill country of Ephraim, life had been hard for twenty years. The landscape was a barren pattern of wasted fields. King Jabin, a Canaanite, had taken all the rich farms in the valley, leaving only the rocky upland pastures for the Hebrews. Most of the crops not destroyed by the heat, the sudden mudslides, and the sandy dirt, Jabin took in payment. Whatever little was left had to last until the next crops came in, a meager harvest the people hid in sacks beneath the stones of their houses.

They could not hope to fight against King Jabin. His general, Sisera, had nine hundred iron chariots at his command, and ten or twenty times the number of troops that the Hebrew army could field. It was no wonder that since the farmers could not fight against Jabin, they had begun to prey upon each other. Neighbors came by night to steal the corn of neighbors. Brothers came before dawn to thieve food from their own brothers.

Whenever Barak thought about the valley, he would shake his head sadly.

He was a great warrior, but he spent little time sharpening his spears these days. He knew the people of Ephraim were powerless against Sisera.

Day after day in the valley was the same: Jabin took more and more land, and the farmers grew more and more angry, and God seemed far away beyond the blue dome that glared down upon the land.

The day that Deborah sent for Barak was like any ordinary day: hot, dusty, with the sun hard and unblinking even now in the early morning. Barak had just come out of his tent and was sitting underneath the flap held up by two tent poles, wondering if Israel had so angered God that He no longer cared whether they lived or died. When he saw the messenger running toward him, the dust from his sandals kicking up into the still air, Barak ducked back into his tent, grabbed the waterskin, and brought it outside. He waited impatiently for the messenger to come, wondering if this was more news about Jabin. But it was not.

"Deborah sends for you," the messenger panted while still a hundred yards away. "Deborah the prophetess calls for you." He came under the shade of the tent flap, his chest heaving.

Barak handed the messenger the waterskin; he needed a moment to think. He had heard of Deborah, the judge who sat under a palm tree in the hill country of Ephraim and handed out wise judgments. It was said that she spoke with the voice of God, and that He had granted her wisdom beyond that of any man in the north country.

"What does Deborah want with me?" Barak asked.

The messenger shrugged his shoulders. The water dripped down his chin. "She calls," was his only answer. "It is enough."

Barak went back into his tent. There would be no grubbing in the ground today. He cleansed his face and hands with water freshened with balsam. He put on his best robe and smoothed oil into his beard. Then he gripped his staff, left the tent, and followed the path left by the messenger, whose feet were already sending puffs of dust into the air as he started back toward the hill country.

What Barak saw along the way darkened his soul. The ground was flinty against his feet, cutting like pottery shards into his soles. How could anyone hope to live in such a land? Perhaps there was no reason for hope. He saw none in the eyes of those he passed. Farmhouses were abandoned, their timbers fallen in. At times he could see a thin farmer railing weakly at his harnessed oxen that dragged a wooden plow through the stones and sand. The children he saw were naked, their bones pushing out against tight skin. He wept as he walked.

When he reached the hill country of Ephraim, he found Deborah under her palm tree, shielded from the hot sun. She was alone, and Barak felt her eyes upon him as he came closer. He did not know where to look, and so he stared back at her. She did not seem disturbed by it.

"Barak, son of Abinoam, the land is troubled."

Barak sat down under the shade of the palm, close to Deborah. "No one can live long in such a place as this."

"The roads are abandoned," she said, "for fear of Sisera, or for fear of thieves. The farmland is dead; the cattle are gone. The people turn to new gods to shield them from the Canaanites."

"What else can they do? God has abandoned His people."

"No!" shouted Deborah abruptly. "Barak, son of Abinoam, you lie."

Barak stared at Deborah. No man would have ever said such a thing to Barak. And certainly no other woman. Who was this Deborah, that she could say such a thing?

"Barak, son of Abinoam, the Lord God commands you to gather ten thousand men together at Mount Tabor."

Barak, stunned, rose to his feet. "There are not that many men in all the north country who would leave their families to come to Tabor. And what would I say to them to make them come?"

"Say that God will bring Sisera to them, with all his troops and all his chariots."

Barak laughed bitterly. "I would not need to tell them that. They would guess it; Jabin would never allow an army to gather. He would send all his nine hundred chariots and his men to cut us to pieces."

But Deborah did not seem to be listening. "God will bring Sisera to you, and you will win a great victory for the Lord."

There was a long silence. The wind rustled the palm fronds overhead, scattering shadow and light on the two.

"How?" Barak finally asked.

Now Deborah stood, and she was angry. Barak saw that she knew his thoughts. He did not trust a woman to give him advice. He did not trust the people to gather at Mount Tabor. And he did not trust a God who seemed to have abandoned His people.

"God will bring Sisera and his army and his chariots to the Kishon River," she answered. "And the battle will be yours."

"How?" Barak asked again. He would brave her anger.

But she would not answer. He stared into her eyes, and when the palm fronds swayed and the light glinted into them, they looked dangerous. It was Barak who finally turned away.

So here was the choice. Barak, one of the greatest warriors among the tribes of Israel, could take the advice of this woman, or return home to his unused spears. He looked far away, over the expanse of hill country, and saw the wasted land left to the people of Ephraim. Perhaps there was no real choice. No one could live without hope.

Barak turned back to Deborah. "I will call for ten thousand men."
She nodded.

"I will hope that they will come."

"They will come," she replied.

"And we will gather at Mount Tabor to meet Sisera."

"And God will give you the victory there," she finished.

"So," said Barak. "But one thing more. One thing more. I will go only if you go with me. If you do not go with me, I will not go."

Deborah sat back down under the palm tree. Now the choice was hers. And again, there was no choice. "I will go with you," she said, "but the honor in this battle will not be yours."

"Let it be yours, then."

"No," she said. "Let it be the Lord's."

So it was that Barak gathered ten thousand men together at Kedesh, and then went on to Mount Tabor. When Jabin heard of this army, he sent Sisera with nine hundred chariots to destroy the Hebrews. But when Sisera crossed the Kishon River, all his soldiers in their iron chariots wallowed in the muddy riverbanks. The Hebrew army avalanched down the mountainside, swords and cries in the air. Terrified, Sisera fled on foot, abandoning his chariot, and Barak and his men destroyed the army of Jabin.

And the honor was the Lord's.

Judges 4:1-16

Gideon and Purah
AT THE MIDIANITE CAMP

It was as dark a night as Purah had ever seen. He was with his master, Gideon, picking his way carefully, quietly among the rocks that littered the valley below the hill of Moreh, spying out the Midianite camp. Spies reported that the Midianites lay as thick as locusts on the valley floor, and that they had more war camels than grains of sand on the side of the sea. But Gideon wanted to see for himself.

Purah chuckled, loudly enough that Gideon looked back at him sharply and silenced him with a wave of his hand. Gideon always wanted to see for himself, Purah thought. He never trusted the messengers who brought news of the Midianite army. He questioned them as one draws juice from a pomegranate, sucking them dry, and then he went out himself to see if the message was true.

Even with God, Purah thought, Gideon always wanted to see for himself.

That first time, under the oak of Ophrah, Gideon knew right away that it was the angel of the Lord sitting beneath the tree. He must have known as soon as the angel greeted him from far away. "The Lord is with you, mighty warrior!" Purah, remembering not to chuckle again, imagined the scene that Gideon later described to him.

"But sir, if the Lord is with me, then why have the Midianites turned Israel to dust? Where are all the wonders that God performed when He brought His people up out of Egypt? Now He has abandoned us." Only Gideon would talk so to an angel.

"Go," the angel replied. "Go in your strength and save Israel from the hand of Midian. I myself will send you."

Gideon scoffed. (How many men, Purah wondered, had scoffed at an angel?) "My clan is the weakest in all of Manasseh, and I am the weakest in my clan."

"Go," the angel repeated. "The Lord will be with you."

Purah imagined Gideon looking slantwise at the angel. He wanted to be sure. He wanted to see for himself.

"If I have found favor with you, and if the Lord is truly with me, then give me a sign that it is really you who are talking to me. Wait here until I come back and bring an offering."

Purah imagined the angel smiling. Surely he had never come across one like this before. "I will wait until you return."

So Gideon ran to his herd and chose a young goat. He cooked its meat, put broth in a pot, baked bread without yeast, and brought all these back to the angel under the oak tree.

"Take the meat and the bread, put them on this rock" — the angel gestured toward a large stone nearby — "and pour the broth over them."

Gideon
and
Purah
at the
Midianite
Camp

—

53

When Gideon had done this, the angel touched the meat and the bread with the tip of his staff, and fire gushed out of the rock, consuming the offering. Purah wondered if the angel smiled at Gideon's surprise before he vanished.

Now Purah saw Gideon signal back at him with his hand, telling him to crouch low. They must be near one of the outposts of the Midianite army. Together they crept closer, staying in the darkest shadows. Soon they were so close that they could see the Midianite soldiers huddled like rocks around the fires. But they were not close enough to hear anything. Gideon signaled that they should move closer.

He wanted to see for himself.

Purah almost chuckled again, even though he was in a valley surrounded by enemies who wanted to kill him. Gideon was always pushing further. He hadn't been satisfied with the angel's fire. After he gathered his army to fight against the Midianites, he tested the Lord again. One evening, he asked Purah to fetch a wool fleece. When he took it, he held it upward toward heaven and prayed aloud. "Lord, if you wish to save Israel by my hand as you have promised, show me now. I will leave this fleece on the threshing floor here. If tomorrow morning there is dew only on the fleece, and if all the ground under it is dry, then I will know that you are the Lord, and that you will save Israel by my hand."

The next morning the fleece was sopping wet with dew, so soaked that it was hard to heft it up. When Gideon lifted it, the dew ran off in streams onto ground that was completely dry.

But Gideon was still not satisfied, and he asked Purah to fetch another fleece. When Purah brought it, Gideon took it and raised it to the heavens again. "This time," he prayed, "let the fleece be dry and the ground wet." In the morning, the Lord had done just as Gideon had asked. Now, finally, Gideon was satisfied.

*Gideon
and
Purah
at the
Midianite
Camp*

—

55

But the Lord was not done.

Gideon gathered together a large army of men, almost as large as the Midianite host. They were camped in the hills surrounding the valley, and when they attacked, it would be with a rush and a surprise that would startle all the Midianites.

But the Lord would now test Gideon. The Lord too would see for Himself.

On the morning before the battle, the Lord told Gideon to send away all those soldiers who were fearful.

Gideon did not question God. "Anyone who trembles with fear may turn back from here," he announced to his army. Purah had watched his face as more than two-thirds of the men dropped their weapons, folded their tents, and left the camps. If Gideon despaired, his face did not show it.

But God was still not done.

"Take the rest of your men down to the water and have them drink," He commanded.

So Gideon did, without question. Most of his men knelt on the banks to drink. But three hundred lifted the water in cupped hands and lapped it up.

"Keep the three hundred," the Lord said. "The rest send home." Again Purah had watched Gideon's face, but Gideon showed nothing. With three hundred men, he would face an army of thousands, but he showed no fear.

And Purah had known that the testing of the Lord was finished.

By now he and Gideon had crept as close to the Midianite camp as they dared. They could hear some nervous laughter and watch the soldiers look over their shoulders up toward the hills and into the darkness behind them. Their spears were close to their sides, and the flickering light of the fires lit up their faces. Gideon and Purah were very quiet and very still.

"I had a dream last night." It was the voice of one of the soldiers. The voice was shaky.

"What was your dream?" asked another.

The first swallowed hard, then spoke slowly. "I dreamed that a round loaf of barley bread came tumbling into our camp. It struck our tent, and the tent collapsed, and we were trapped in it."

The second swore. "This can mean only one thing. The God of Gideon has given us and the whole camp into his hand. What should we do?"

Gideon tapped Purah's shoulder, and they backed away into the darkness. Crouching low, they headed back up into the hills, and when they were out of earshot, Purah heard Gideon humming a psalm of praise to God. When they were far enough away that they could not be seen by the outposts, Gideon put his arm around Purah's shoulder. "The Lord has given them into my hand, just as He said He would."

Before morning broke that day, Gideon returned with his three hundred men. They set themselves on all sides of the camp, each man with a sword strapped to his waist and carrying a trumpet in one hand and a flaming torch hidden in a clay jar in the other. At Gideon's signal, Purah blew his trumpet, and three hundred more sounded. Then each man smashed his jar, rushed toward the camp with his lighted torch, and shouted — so loudly that the stars rang with it — "A sword for the Lord and for Gideon!" The Midianites, confused and terrified, began fighting each other to find a way to escape, and the back of the Midianite army was broken.

Gideon saw it for himself.

Judges 6 : 1 – 7 : 2 2

Samson

IN THE TEMPLE OF DAGON

He felt the cold stone curving under his hands, pillars on either side of him that rose and rose and rose in the great temple of Dagon. He pushed, testing to see if his shoulders would bear the weight that they had once borne so easily, so thoughtlessly. But they would not.

"Push harder, Samson," called a voice, drunk with purple wine. "We are all trembling at the sight of your sinews." Guffaws filled the temple.

"Is this the Samson that we once feared?"

"Get him a donkey's jawbone. Maybe he can do something with that."

"Perhaps we should bring him to Gaza's gates!"

More laughter. Samson felt a piece of wet fruit smack against his chest.

"His God has abandoned him." A female voice that time, one he recognized.

Abandoned. His chains weighed down his arms, and he trembled at the strain of holding them up. Abandoned. If he could have called out to them, he would have proclaimed that God does not abandon those who cling to Him — but his voice was parched with the thirst of long imprisonment. If he could have rushed at them, he would have wrung their necks — but he was chained. If he could have looked at them, he would have stared down their laughter — but he was blinded.

And the thirst and the chains and the gore that ran down his face into his beard said, together, one thing: Abandoned. Abandoned by God. Abandoned.

How could it have come to this?

There was a time when it had not been so. Over the voices that swirled around him, he heard his mother's voice crooning to him and telling him the wonderful story of the day in Mahaneh-dan when the angel of the Lord had come to her. "I did not know who he was, but he told me that I would have a child, even though I had not been able to have children. And he told me it would be a boy. You," she said, with the light laughter that he remembered so well.

And Samson could hear his own voice asking, "And what happened then?" even though he could tell the story almost as well as she.

She would smile and tell him again. "He told me not to take any wine or any drink that had fermented, and he told me not to eat anything unclean. And after he had told me these things a second time, when your father was with me, your father and I offered up a goat to the Lord, and when the fire blazed to heaven, the angel stepped into it and went up."

"And that is when you knew he was an angel."

"Yes, that is when we knew."

"And he told you why I had been born."

"Yes, he told us."

"To free our people from the Philistines."

And at this his mother would look troubled.

All his life, Samson had known that he was to free his people from the Philistines. And now here he was in their chains, pushing weak arms against stone pillars.

"Samson," called another voice from the temple. "Here's a riddle:

> *Out of the eater, something to eat;*
> *Out of the strong, something sweet.*"

The crowd roared; they had heard this before.

"Do you remember the answer, Samson? Or perhaps we can come up with a better one. Maybe you're the answer. From the strong Samson comes sweet vengeance for the Philistines."

Samson remembered the riddle; he had posed it himself. It had led to his first betrayal, from which he had learned nothing.

He flexed his hands, remembering how the lion had felt under them. He remembered how it had bounded toward him, snarling, in the vineyards of Timnah. He remembered the first moment of panic, and then the strength that had flowed into him suddenly, the strength that the Lord had given him as His blessing. It had been nothing for him to kill the lion, because he had done it with the Lord's strength. And then he knew how he was to deliver his people from the hands of the Philistines.

It had been a long time since he had gone to Timnah, the home of the woman he had married. He could almost feel the bitterness of Timnah's ground under his feet. The lion that he had killed would be only a skeleton now. And the bees that he had found in its carcass and the honey that he had taken from it were probably gone as well. But the memory of the riddle was

not. "Out of the strong, something sweet" — out of the lion, honey. He had
posed the riddle to thirty Philistines on his wedding day and wagered thirty
linen garments and thirty festive garments that they could not solve it. For
four days they could not answer, and never would have been able to if Samson
had not given in to the wheedling of his new wife and told her about the lion.
She had given the answer to the men.

And they had all paid dearly since that betrayal. Samson, enraged, had
gone down to Ashkelon, killed thirty Philistines, and used their clothing to pay
off his wager. His father-in-law, thinking that Samson no longer wanted his
daughter — and perhaps afraid that he did — gave her to another. Samson
replied by burning the fields and olive groves of the Philistines. The Philistines
answered by murdering the woman who had been his wife, as well as her
father. And Samson had sought out and slaughtered the murderers.

Had he spilled all this blood to deliver Israel from the Philistines? Or had
he spilled it for his own pleasure? How had everything spiraled out of control
so quickly? How had he come to be the prisoner of these chains? How had he
been abandoned?

Perhaps he had been the one to do the abandoning.

Samson shook his head sadly. The blessing that God had given him so
freely, so freely, he had tossed away like water into the sand. God had given
him his strength to lead his people; he had known that once. He had known
that the day his own people had come to bind him and give him over to the
Philistines, fearing what the Philistines would do to their towns if they would
not hand him over. And Samson had gone, confident in God. And the Lord
had not abandoned him.

When Samson had appeared in the Philistine camp, bound by two new
ropes, the Philistines had cheered and rushed toward him, swords out.
Hundreds of men coming to kill him. And the Lord had sent His strength to

Samson. The ropes had fallen from him like charred reeds. He had picked up a jawbone from a mess of nearby bones that had once been a donkey, and he had swung it against the Philistines. In the Lord's strength, he had killed a thousand of Israel's enemies, and the rest had fled in terror.

When the people of Israel saw this thing, they knew that the Lord was in Samson. So they had followed him for twenty years, and in that time he had raided camps, carried off city gates, and spread terror among the invaders. Israel had not abandoned him, and the strength of the Lord had filled him.

But then had come the day in the Valley of Sorek when he had met Delilah. The beautiful Delilah. She had reminded him of the wife he had lost. He did not know how much alike they were. Now he could hardly understand how he could have missed it all so completely. How was it that he had not seen her coming betrayal?

The Philistines had bribed her to betray him. If you can discover the secret of his great strength, they had said, we will make you wealthy beyond your dreams. It was nothing to her to give Samson away. "Tell me the secret of your strength," she had demanded one night, playfully. And he had laughed.

"If anyone ties me with seven fresh bowstrings that have never been dried in the sun, I will become as weak as any man." He had laughed at her smile then, and he had laughed the next day when she tied him up and then called out in terror that the Philistines were upon him. He burst the bowstrings as easily as a candle burns through twine. Delilah pouted.

"You made a fool of me. You say you love me, but you do not trust me. Come, tell me how you may be tied."

Samson thought quickly. He had always liked posing riddles. "If you tied me with ropes that have never been used, then I would become as weak as any man." So the next night she tied him with new ropes, and she again called out that the Philistines had come upon him, and again Samson broke free, snapping off the ropes as if they were no more than thread.

More pouting from Delilah. More tears. More wheedling. And still he had not seen what was coming. "Samson, you have been fooling with me. Tell me how you may be tied."

"If you weave the seven braids of my hair into the fabric on your loom, and if you tighten it all with a pin, then I will be as weak as any man."

Samson had not been surprised when he woke the next day to Delilah's cries: "The Philistines are upon you, Samson!" But he again broke free, scattering the loom.

After that, a song of pain and accusation became Delilah's daily chant. She sang it to Samson in the morning: "How can you say 'I love you' when you do not?" She sang it to him at noon: "You will not trust me because you do not love me." And she sang it to him during the cold nights: "If you love me, you will tell me your secret."

Finally, worn down by her constant complaints, Samson told her the truth. "My hair," he explained, "has never been cut. It is a sign that I am dedicated to the Lord. If it was to be cut, the Lord would abandon me, and I would be as weak as any man." How could he not have known what would happen next?

When morning came and Delilah shouted once again that the Philistines had come, Samson rose from his bed and found lying around him the braids of his hair. His head had been shaved. And this time the Philistines were indeed upon him.

They bound him, dragged him by the heels out of his house, and threw him into a damp dungeon. He shuddered, remembering what the jailors did to him before they tied him to a mill wheel and forced him to grind their grain. But his hair began to grow again.

Now, in the temple of Dagon, the chains grew heavier on Samson's arms, the pillars colder to his hands. Around him the laughter grew louder, the music wilder, the jeers coarser. Then suddenly it grew quiet; someone had stood to speak.

"Our god is stronger than the God of the Israelites," proclaimed a deep voice. "Dagon brought our enemy into our hands, the one who burned our fields and murdered our people. Dagon humbled this Samson, and humbled his God."

And suddenly Samson knew something so surely that it tightened his chest. He wanted to tell the Philistines that God does not abandon those who cling to Him. But why could he not tell this thing to himself? In his fear and guilt, he had been afraid to cling to God. With that thought, Samson knew that God had never left him. And he was no longer afraid.

"O Lord," he prayed quietly. "Remember me, your foolish servant Samson. Remember me as you remembered me in the days of my youth."

One by one, the Philistines turned to Samson, listening to his prayer. Their laughter died away.

"Remember me now, and let me bring judgment upon the Philistines. And let it be, Lord, that this day I come into your kingdom."

Samson braced his hands against the pillars. Into his shoulders spread the strength of the Lord, the strength that had stirred in him in Mahaneh-dan, the strength given him in the vineyards of Timnah, in the city of Gaza, and now in the very temple of the pagan god.

"Hear, O Israel, the Lord our God, the Lord is One," he shouted, and pushed.

Judges 13:2–16:30

The Calling of Samuel

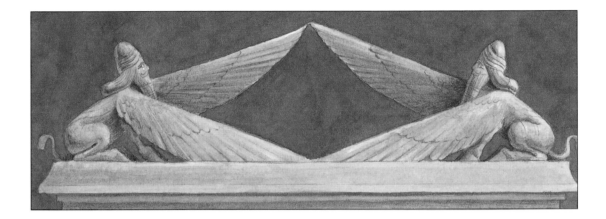

Samuel had served in the Temple before the Lord God ever since he could remember, but never before had he been as frightened as he was this night. He lay still, hardly daring to move, and thought of his mother.

Every year his mother came to tell him the story of how he had come to the Temple. And every year he listened as though the story was brand new. Hannah told him of her prayer that she might have a son. She told him how God had sent Samuel to her, and how she had promised to dedicate him to the Lord and have him serve in the Temple.

Afterward, Samuel helped his father make the annual sacrifice, wearing the new robe that Hannah brought each year. Then he walked with them to the Temple porch, helped them gather his five brothers and sisters like hens gathering their chicks, and watched them set off back home. He would not see them for another year.

After these visits, the old priest Eli left Samuel alone for the rest of the day.

Most days in the Temple — not this day, but most days — were the same. The routines of the Temple had grown familiar. Besides assisting at the annual sacrifices, Samuel carried out daily tasks: he folded the sleeping mats, swept the floors, helped Eli dress in his fine vestments, cleansed the sacrificial blood from the Temple floors, and studied. But he kept one task until last: tending the lamp of God. In front of the curtain that separated the Holy of Holies from the rest of the Temple, he poured the oil, cleaned the wick, and knew that he was near God Himself.

Eli performed some of these same tasks — though he would never fold the mats or sweep the floors. But Samuel sensed that Eli did these things like a man who had nothing else to do until he died and the tasks ended. Samuel wondered if Eli ever felt his fingers tingle when he approached the curtain that shielded the Holy of Holies. He wondered if Eli kept his eyes down when he came near the Ark of the Lord. He wondered if Eli felt God's eye on him when he prayed, or if he felt God's presence when he slit the white lamb's throat and spilled its life on the altar. Sometimes, when Samuel watched a sacrifice, he felt as if the room were so stuffed with God's greatness that it pressed against his chest, so that when the blood flowed down the altar he could hardly breathe. He wondered if Eli felt that.

But this night, Samuel was afraid. Eli was asleep in his chamber. He had asked Samuel to tend the lamp of God until it went out. But for some reason, it did not go out. As the night wore on, Samuel fetched his own sleeping mat, took off the linen ephod he wore and folded it carefully by his feet, and lay down outside the Holy of Holies. He watched the light play against the beaten gold of the walls and tried not to think of the presence of God so close to his mat.

The lamplight never dimmed; the oil never ran out. It burned brightly in the darkness, and then sparked when suddenly a voice called out, softly, as if trying to wake a beloved one from sleep: "Samuel!"

Samuel sat up, startled. Wrapping his arms around his chest to ward off the cold, he ran to Eli's chamber. "Here I am," he said to Eli, shaking him gently by the shoulder. "You called me."

Eli looked at him, trying to focus his eyes through sleep. "I did not call," he said grumpily. "You're dreaming, boy. Go back to sleep."

Samuel thought the sound of his own feet padding back through the Temple halls, toward the Holy of Holies, was surprisingly loud. He lay back down again, wondering why the lamp of God was still burning.

"Samuel!" The voice again! Samuel was certain now that Eli was calling him. Perhaps the first time had been a dream, but not now. He ran back to Eli, shivering.

"Here I am," he called again.

Eli looked at him, exasperated. "Boy, I did not call you. Go back to bed. Go back to bed and do not wake this old man again."

Puzzled, Samuel went back to his mat. He decided that he would stay awake and listen. But the dancing light on the walls lulled him to sleep.

"Samuel!" There could be no doubt that someone was calling him, and Eli was the only one within the Temple. Samuel hesitated, but then ran once again to Eli's side.

"Here I am!" This time he expected that Eli might be angry. Or that he might be genuinely puzzled. Or that perhaps he would break out laughing because he was playing a joke on Samuel. But what happened was the one thing that Samuel did not expect. Eli began to cry.

"Were you called again?" he asked Samuel.

"Yes."

"And was it the same voice?"

Samuel nodded his head.

Eli wiped his face with the back of his hand. "Go back and lie down. When you hear the voice again, say, 'Speak, Lord. Your servant listens.'"

"But who is calling me?"

Eli turned on his side, his face away from Samuel. "It is the Lord God who calls you," he said, his voice filled with a longing that brought tears to Samuel's own eyes. "Now go back and lie down."

Trembling, but not from the cold, Samuel went back into the Holy of Holies and lay down on his sleeping mat. The lamp glowed even more brightly than before. He lay awake, waiting for the voice of God. When it came, he jerked upright and covered his face with his hands.

"Samuel! Samuel!"

"Speak, Lord. Your servant listens."

The voice came, filled with stern gladness, like a trumpet announcing jubilee.

"I am about to do something in Israel that will make the ears of everyone who hears of it tingle." Samuel felt his own ears tingling, and he bowed his head still further.

"The day of Eli the high priest and his sons is over, for his sons have done blasphemy against me, and he has not restrained them. You will be my prophet. All Israel, from Dan to Beersheba, will know you as the prophet of the Lord." Samuel began to weep, and when the voice stopped speaking, the lamp went out, and Samuel was alone in the darkness.

Later, when the sounds that filtered through the curtain told Samuel that the new day had come, he rose and put on his ephod, and over it he put the robe his mother had given him. Shouldering the hard blessing of God, he went out to meet Eli.

1 Samuel 3:1-20

THE SHIELD BEARER OF Goliath

When the shield bearer woke, he prayed the same prayer to the same gods that he had been praying for well over a month: "Let this be the last day!"

The prayer was never answered.

He lay in his cot until he heard Goliath's roar. He knew what he would have to do in response. First he would fetch the food — the cook would not come near the giant's tent — and serve it to the foul-smelling monster, trying hard not to show his disgust. Then he would arm the giant, wrapping leather around the festered skin where the armor's rough edges rubbed the flesh raw. Then the bearer would bring the spear and the sword, the huge shield, the great bronze helmet, the greaves for his legs, and the scaled chest plate, lugging them from around the back of the tent, preparing the giant to meet the enemy. Finally, he would lead the giant — keeping him downwind, if possible — to the edge of the battlefield, facing the Hebrew army.

If only today would be the last day.

He never spoke with the giant. No one did. The giant gave them no reason to. The first day he had come to camp, the soldiers scurried out of the way, half in disgust, half in fear. He had gone into his tent without speaking to anyone, and the metal-workers had fired their forges to prepare his armor and weapons. No one had seen him again until the next morning, when he ripped open a flap of his tent and pointed to one of them. "You will be the shield bearer," he had said, and the soldier could not protest. He was in the wrong place at the wrong time, and he was sure no one else would volunteer. That very day his prayers began.

In a way, the bearer could almost — almost — feel sorrow for Goliath. Day after day, morning and evening, he walked to the edge of the field, cried out to the Hebrews across the valley, and then returned to drink and eat and sleep in his tent. The army would cheer behind him while he sent his boasts across the way, but once he was finished, he would return to his tent in silence, sneering even at his allies. The bearer wondered if there was ever anyone the giant did not sneer at. He wondered if Goliath had ever sat by a fire to tell stories, or looked up at the stars to make pictures of them, or fought side by side with someone that he cared for. He doubted it.

The giant's life was boasting, eating, and sleeping. The bearer wondered how Goliath could live at all. Sometimes he doubted whether there was even a soul buried beneath the monstrous flesh.

This day began like the forty others before it since the giant had come to camp: the roar, the food, the armor, the march to the edge of the field, the army crowding — upwind — behind the giant, cheering his calls. The bearer stood beside and a little in front of the giant, holding the shield that the giant would use if an enemy dared to challenge his boasts. He peered across the valley of Elah at the tents of the Hebrews, knowing that nothing would be any different. No man would come to fight the monster.

"Why do you not line up for battle?" the monster challenged. "Why do you pitch your tents and do nothing? Are you not Saul's men, and I a Philistine? Come to battle, or better yet, choose a champion. He and I will fight in the valley between the two armies. The army of the one who is killed will serve the champion's king."

No sound from the Hebrew camp. It was one of those hot, still mornings, so quiet that you could hear the water falling off the rocks in the brook at the valley's bottom. The shield bearer began to grow thirsty. He wondered how much longer the boasting would go on.

"This day I defy Israel and its God. Give me a man to fight — if you have one!"

Still no sound. The tents on the other side of the field may as well have been deserted; only the slow smoke of the cooking fires showed that anyone was there. The shield bearer did not blame the Hebrews for hiding in their tents. With a grunt the giant turned to go, and the bearer turned with him. The giant was sneering, but the bearer was tired. Give him a good battle anytime. Or at least someone that he could serve honorably. But this monster . . .

Suddenly the Philistine army quieted, and the bearer turned around. Across the valley — could this be possible? — a boy was coming out from the tents, wearing no armor, holding only a staff and what appeared to be a small slingshot. He must be a messenger. But if so, he was acting strangely. He stopped briefly at the brook and bent down, put something from it in his pouch, and then came on toward them, as determined as if he were an army himself.

The wind picked up.

The sneer grew deeper on the monster's face, but the bearer did not notice. He saw only the boy coming toward them, confident, as if he would not fear facing a lion. His skin had taken on the sun's heat, the mountain's wind, the night's cool. For a moment the bearer thought — wildly — of throwing down his shield and rushing to him. Here would be someone to serve.

"Am I a dog," the monster called over the head of the boy, "that you send me this babe carrying sticks?" The giant singed the air with his curses, with all the hatred and loneliness that filled his guts. But there was no response from the Hebrew tents. And still the boy advanced. And still the wind grew stronger.

"Boy," called the giant, speaking to him for the first time, "this day you die. I will give your flesh to the birds of the air and your blood to the beasts of the field."

The boy said nothing. He came on.

The giant grunted in surprise. The shield bearer did not turn around, but he knew that if he did, he might see something different in the monster's face.

"By all the gods that terrify this earth," the monster called, "I will kill you." The bearer heard the coarse steel of the giant's sword grate against its scabbard as the giant drew it out.

The boy was now close. He set his staff down, held his slingshot in one hand, and with the other reached into the shepherd's bag by his side. The bearer could not see what he took out. And then he spoke, and his voice was strong and unafraid.

"The battle is not yours. The battle is the Lord's. You come with spear and sword and shield. I come in the name of the Lord God Almighty. This day He will hand you to me, and the birds of the air and the beasts of the field will indeed come to feed." Whatever he had taken from his pouch, he fixed it in his slingshot and began to swing it overhead. "This day the whole world will know that the God of Israel is God of all."

The bearer trembled, and he did not know why. He could feel the hot

anger of the giant behind him; no one had ever spoken to him this way, no one in his entire life. The wind frenzied around them now, blowing directly out of the Hebrew camp, blowing open the tent flaps where the soldiers of Israel stood, watching the champion of their God.

At the same moment that the giant hefted his sword high into the air — the bearer could see the shadow of it stretching across the ground and reaching out to the boy — the boy loosed his slingshot so that a stone flew out of it like a bird that knew its roost. From the moment the stone left the slingshot, the bearer knew that it carried death. He did not have to see it hit the giant; he knew it would. The boy had said so.

The world slowed. The wind dropped. The cries of the Philistine army stilled. And in the utter quiet of the moment, the bearer heard the thudding of the stone into bone, saw the shadow of the sword fall, and felt the earth quiver at the weight of the body that fell beside him. The bearer turned and looked into the giant's face, smeared with blood and dust, and saw the eyes dulling into death. The sneer was gone, and in its place — a pleading.

The bearer threw down the shield, tore off his helmet, and fled toward the dissolving Philistine lines. He did not look back at the boy, or at the triumphant Hebrew soldiers pursuing his army. He ran through the day and long into the night. And when a heavy rain came to close him off from the others who were fleeing, he sat behind a boulder and wept for what might have been.

1 Samuel 17:1-50

Elijah and Elisha

AT THE JORDAN RIVER

When they left Gilgal together, Elisha knew that this was to be his last journey with his master, Elijah. He could not bear to think about that. He would not let himself think about that. Instead, he asked Elijah to tell the stories one more time.

"On Mount Carmel," Elisha began.

"On Mount Carmel I faced the prophets of Baal, and God defeated them." As Elijah spoke, Elisha saw the four hundred and fifty priests of Baal weeping and screaming and wailing and cutting themselves, praying for their god to send down fire from heaven to consume their sacrifice. And after nothing happened, Elijah doused his offering with bucket after bucket of water made precious by the drought, until it streamed from the sacrifice and filled the trench around the altar. Only then did God send His fire.

"At the ravine of Cherith," started Elisha.

"At the ravine of Cherith," continued Elijah, "I learned that God would always be with me." And he told of the brook that he drank from, and the ravens who each morning and each evening brought him bread and meat, so that he did not die of hunger or thirst during the drought, while he hid from King Ahab.

"And at Zarephath . . ."

"At Zarephath I learned that God will always provide." And Elijah told of the widow who was able to feed him and her family because her jar of flour was never used up and her jug of oil never ran dry, until God finally sent rain to the parched land.

The stories kept Elisha from weeping as they walked. At first, Elijah had not wanted Elisha to come with him. At Gilgal, he had told him to stay behind. "The Lord has sent me to Bethel," Elijah had said. "Stay here."

Elisha did not know if he was to stay because the Lord commanded it, or if Elijah thought this would make their parting less painful. But Elisha would have none of it. "As surely as the Lord lives and you live, I will not leave you," he said. And so the two had gone on to Bethel together.

As they walked down to Bethel, Elisha could see that God had blessed the land. The olive groves had grown so fully that the trees spread their boughs over each side of the road, so that for a time the two men walked in cool green light. In the vineyards, the vines were just beginning to sag under the weight of the green grapes; the harvest would be good. Sheep ran their sheepy runs against the wet green of the hills. And the fields of grain, just beginning to turn golden under the late summer sun, reached to where the sky dropped itself down to the land like a tent stretched and pegged to the ground. There was a freshness deep down in the world.

If Elisha had not known that this was his last time with Elijah, this bounty and beauty would have made him glad. As it was, he tried not to think about what would soon happen.

But at Bethel he was reminded of what he and Elijah were doing. The prophets there came out to meet them, all eager to tell Elisha the terrible news. "Do you know that the Lord is going to take your master from you today?"

Elisha looked at them with sorrowed eyes. "I know. Do not speak of it."

Elijah felt Elisha's pain in his soul. "Elisha," he said gently, his hand old but strong on his elbow, "Elisha, God has sent me to Jericho. Stay here."

Elisha shook his head. "As surely as the Lord lives and you live, I will not leave you." So they went on together to Jericho.

When they reached that city, the prophets there gathered around when they saw Elijah. "Do you know," they asked Elisha, "that the Lord is going to take your master from you today?"

Elisha looked angrily at them. "I know. Do not speak of it."

Elijah felt Elisha's anger in his soul. "Elisha," he said, "the Lord has sent me to the Jordan River. Stay here."

"As surely as the Lord lives and you live, I will not leave you." So they went on together to the Jordan River, with fifty of the prophets following behind them.

When the two reached the Jordan, the prophets stood at a distance from them, watching. Elisha, head bowed, could not bear to have them so near, and Elijah knew this in his soul. So he took off his cloak, rolled it up, and struck the water. Immediately the current hesitated, then stopped at the place it was struck while the rest of the water ran downriver. Elijah and Elisha walked across the dry path of riverbed, leaving the prophets behind. When they had crossed to the other side, the current surged back, frothing by the shore.

That, at least, brought a smile to Elisha's face.

But now it was time to part. There was no need to say much. Everything had been said long ago.

Elijah took Elisha by the elbow once more. "Is there anything else I can do for you before I am taken?" he asked. "Tell me."

Behind them the Jordan River lazed past, its clear waters pushing the pebbles along the shore. It was hard for Elisha to believe that soon the river would go on flowing, pushing those pebbles, but that Elijah would be gone from the world. The olives would be pressed, the grapes picked, the grain scythed, and Elijah would be harvested along with them.

"Only one thing," Elisha replied. "Let the spirit of God that dwells in you be twice as strong in me. Without that, I cannot be God's prophet."

Elijah nodded, pleased. "You ask a hard thing. And a hard thing is asked of you. I cannot say whether God will grant your request. But this I do know: If you see me taken up, your prayer will be answered."

All this time, the fifty prophets had been standing on the far side of the Jordan, watching Elisha and Elijah; the two had felt the fifty pairs of eyes on their backs. So they walked on through the heated air, feeling the afternoon sun burning down on them, until Elisha did not know whether his face was wet from the sweat of his forehead or from tears. Their path took them behind a low hill, away from the river, and as soon as they could no longer hear the sounds of the water, the air grew still and even hotter. It seemed to yellow around them, until the stillness burst with a blast of wind as if from a furnace.

And then, thundering down the steps of the sky, riding the flaming air, two fiery horses pulled a chariot hot with the winds of the sun. It surged between the two men, throwing Elisha to the ground. And as the wind swirled the dust into a great whirlwind up in the air, Elijah, never looking back, stepped into the chariot and gripped its sides as the horses pawed up the whirlwind into the sky.

"My father, my father! The chariots and horsemen of Israel!" Elisha cried. But there was no answer.

He knelt on the ground, his face in his hands, and wept.

And then, fluttering down from the sky like a bird looking for a place to land, Elijah's brown cloak fell near Elisha. Elisha picked it up; it was cool and heavy. He stood and wrapped it around himself. Then he turned back to the river.

On the other side of the Jordan, the prophets were still waiting. Elisha saw them watching him come on alone, wearing Elijah's cloak.

When he reached the shore, he stood for a moment, feeling very alone. He had seen Elijah caught up. But had his prayer been answered? He shrugged the cloak back from his shoulders and rolled it up. "Lord of Elijah," he prayed, "are you here with me now?" Then he struck the waters of the Jordan.

The current hesitated, then stopped at the place it was struck while the rest of the water ran downriver. Elisha walked across the dry path of riverbed, and when he stepped onto the farther bank, the current surged back, frothing by the shore.

Elisha set out toward Jericho and the work that God had readied for him.

1 Kings 17:1-16
18:16-38
2 Kings 2:1-14

King Darius
WAITS FOR DANIEL

ing Darius stood on the private porch of his palace, rubbing his signet ring back and forth against his leg. Across the broad courtyard came roars from the lions' den that were at first terrible, and then very quiet. *They are feeding now,* he thought, and the image made his stomach turn.

But what else could he have done? The satraps had tricked him — again. A silly law. He had signed it for no reason other than to satisfy his vanity: "No one shall pray to any god or man except to King Darius — May he live forever! — for the next thirty days. Anyone who disobeys shall be thrown into the den of lions." At the time, King Darius wondered why the punishment was included. It was not usually done.

Now he knew why. He had not known how much his satraps had hated Daniel.

Dawn drew close now. Already the graying sky had faded some of the stars, and Darius could begin to make out housetops against the darkness. The tinkling sounds of the hand cymbals still chinged their cold sounds in the palace hall below him; the satraps were celebrating right through the night. No one knew that King Darius stood here, alone, waiting for daybreak so that he could rush to the lions' den and have the stone at the mouth of the den rolled away, the stone sealed by the mark of his own signet ring.

The lions were still quiet. Darius could remember some dawns when the lions, hungry through the night, had roared the morning into light, waking him with their pain and hunger and anger. But not so today. If he had not known what he would find in that den when it was opened, he could almost have felt at peace.

He laughed, a flat and horrible laugh. Was peace something that a king could ever have? Once he had thought it was possible — when he had met Daniel, one of the exiled Jews. At first the king had laughed at Daniel's earnestness. Daniel still thought that someday his God would return His people to their land. But it wasn't long before Darius was no longer laughing. He had found Daniel wise in ways that none of his counselors were. Daniel knew more of the world than all of his magicians. He could interpret dreams that baffled his wisest men. He had read the writing on the wall that no one else had been able to interpret.

All this — but even more. In a world where justice went to the highest bidder, where the king's officials advanced as they became more skilled in cheating those around them, Daniel was an honest man. Darius had seen the satraps sneer at that honesty. He had heard them laugh at Daniel's ways. Sometimes he had even laughed with them.

But there came a day when King Darius envied Daniel. It was not an easy thing for him to admit. A king should never envy a slave. But he did. He envied Daniel's knowledge of God's presence. How often had he prayed to the gods, offered sacrifices, stood in the scented smoke without breathing, waiting for the spirit of the gods to fill him. And how often had he come away knowing that he was waiting for a response from something as lifeless as the stone it was made of.

But not so for Daniel. Not so. He prayed to his God whenever he could; he prayed to One who knew him. Darius could see that, even if all of his satraps sneered. Daniel knew God — and what was more, Daniel was known by God. And so Darius envied him.

The satraps also envied Daniel, but not for his relationship with his God. They envied him his position. He had started as a slave, but Darius, still new to his own position, had recognized Daniel for what he was. Soon he had made Daniel a satrap, and then one of the three nobles set over the satraps, and then the first of the three nobles, the highest-ranking official in the kingdom after Darius himself. Even if one of the satraps had risen this high, the others would have been envious. But for a slave to reach this position! For a Jewish exile with no country to his name! Darius smiled to himself, remembering how the satraps had struggled to suppress the rage in their faces when he had made the announcement.

He should have known that they would plot against Daniel. Belshazzar, the king before Darius, would have guessed. But Darius himself had not been king long enough to understand how the court seethed and boiled beneath him.

So now he stood on his private porch, waiting for the dawn to break so that he could go to the lions' den and weep over the shredded body of his . . . friend.

If only Daniel's God was greater than the stone idols he himself prayed to. If only Daniel was right. But Darius was no longer sure that any God ruled. If there was a God, nothing like this could ever happen.

The western horizon was dragging down the last stars, and the east was blushing like one of the girls who carried ices into his rooms. The outline of the houses surrounding the palace now showed distinctly, and the chinging sounds from the palace had hushed. The light grew, first orange and then pink and then, in a flash, bright white, the dawn of his first day without Daniel.

And still the lions were quiet.

But Darius was quiet no longer.

He hurried out of the palace through a private passageway, avoiding the usual attentions made over his departure. When he reached the lions' den, he quickly motioned the guards over, pointing to the stone. They broke the seal that he had set there with his own ring and, flexing their shoulders, set themselves to roll away the stone from the place where Darius expected to see death.

"Daniel!" Darius cried before the stone was fully away. "Daniel, has your God rescued you?" The last words caught in his throat. He was sure that the only thing that would come out of the den would be the roaring of lions.

"Yes, O my king. God has saved me."

Darius stood as still as stone. The guards looked at each other, then into the den, then back at each other. In all their years, such a thing had never happened. Immediately Darius commanded that Daniel be brought out of the den, and the guards, still awestruck, hefted him out. When Darius looked down, the lions lay in a corner, heaped on top of one another, calmly licking their paws and yawning like dogs just waking up.

"Daniel!" said Darius, clapping him on the shoulders. "Daniel, you have served your God without stopping. And now he has done this great thing for you. No other god could have done this thing."

"You are right," agreed Daniel. "No other god could have done this. The Lord sent His angel to shut the mouths of the lions. They could not hurt me, because the Lord held me close. All my life I have tried to serve Him, and now He has saved me." Darius held Daniel close, like a brother. It was something the guards would never see again. The king, decked out in purple silks, embracing a prisoner. It was hard to say which was the greater miracle. The air was heavy with the mystery of it.

"Daniel," whispered Darius finally, "the king that had you for a counselor, and your God as his God, could bring peace to his land."

Daniel bowed his head. "All my life I will try to serve you, my lord."

That very day King Darius sat down at the royal desk and, with Daniel standing by his side, issued this decree:

All those in all parts of my kingdom, reverence and fear the God of Daniel. He is the living God, who lives forever, whose kingdom can never be destroyed. He rescues and he saves. He performs wonders in the heavens and on earth. No other god may stand before him.

And when the scribe had finished writing the decree, Darius stamped it with his own signet ring.

Daniel 5:31 – 6:28

Jonah
HEADS TO TARSHISH

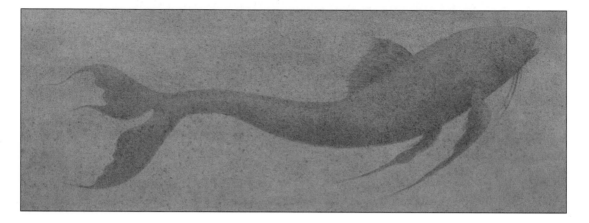

The captain should have seen the clouds as a sign, he told himself later. It had started out as a perfect day to set sail: clear sky, bright sun, gentle winds. He had his crewmen load the ship with the cargo intended for Tarshish — even let the merchants board. And then the gray clouds began boiling up on the horizon. Every one of his sailor's instincts told him that he should postpone the voyage, stay safely tied up at Joppa's piers.

But then this man, this Jonah, came slinking onto the ship, the hood of his cloak drawn over his head, promising so much payment for his passage to Tarshish that the captain knew he must be a fugitive trying to escape from someone. The captain had carried fugitives before, stowing them below deck, behind the wine and the wheat that commanded such high prices. But never had he been offered this much.

And still he hesitated, looking at the sky. "Those clouds," he said, pointing, "show a storm."

"There is much more than a storm in those clouds," Jonah replied as he pulled his hood down even further. Then he handed the captain a heavy, clinking pouch and hurried on board. The weight of the pouch made up the captain's mind.

Still, he felt strangely suspicious of his new passenger. Even in the confusion and ordered chaos of getting underway, the captain's eyes kept straying to the fugitive — to his dark figure huddling behind a group of merchants on deck. It was almost as if he feared he was being watched. Strange.

Just an hour into the voyage, the clouds began to look as if they were following the ship. They scuttled out across the water from the east — in exactly the direction they should not have come from. At first the captain thought he could outrun them, and he had the crew set forward sails. With a calm authority he sent the passengers below — all of them, that is, except Jonah. He had already gone skulking down into the hold, having spent most of his time on deck staring not at the mounting waves but at the sky. Very strange.

The captain kept the sails on even when the wind began to pick up, threatening to tatter them. But it wasn't long before he realized that there was no chance of outrunning this storm. He had the sails brought in and put his best man on the rudder.

The captain wasn't afraid then. He had weathered many a storm. But he had not counted on a wave cutting across the grain of the seas. He had seen these before, of course — waves coming from a direction you could never predict. Usually they never came with much left in them, having been battered by the rhythm of the waves running before the wind. But this one had more than enough left in it to splinter the rudder and send the ship spinning out of control.

Desperately, the captain tried to think, tried to blot out the wind, the piling waves, the furtive figure of Jonah that lurked in his mind. He could not steer by sail; even if they could set a sail, a wind like this would tear it from the mast in seconds. He could not repair the rudder — not in seas like this. But he could make the ship lighter so that it would ride higher.

He sent a crewman to the aft hold to see how deep the water was. A storm like this would twist the seams and open up the pitch, so he wasn't surprised to hear that the water was up to the crewman's knees and coming in fast. "Send six men aft to bail and six forward!" he shouted.

But the storm did not let up. It swirled around and grew stronger, so that the screaming of the wind and the cracks of thunder tore into the captain's bones. Every wave crested above the masthead. Every wave. It was only by a miracle that they slid out from the trough and slipped over the crest before the white water buried them.

A crewman was shouting at him against the wind — something about the water. He knew it was time for the next step. "Start on the cargo!" he called. "Make sure you unload it evenly."

So his crew had started to drag up the sacks of grain, the bolts of cloth, the clay jars of red wine. And they had dragged up the fat merchants with them, the ones who had pushed and shoved to get below before the rains came. Now some stood looking sick, their faces gray and pinched. Some screamed up at the captain and waved their hands toward their goods being fed to the waves. And some dropped to their knees, praying to the gods that they might be saved. It was hard to believe that the gods could possibly hear through the wind and the thunder that broke the air above them.

The captain watched for Jonah, wondering if he would be screaming or praying. But Jonah did not come up from the hold.

Suddenly a wave snapped off the center mast, cleanly and easily, tossing it into the water and skewing the ship around. "Clear away! Clear away!" screamed the captain, and the crew rushed with knives to sever the ropes that still tied the mast to the ship. The drag of it would keep the boat from cresting the waves, and already more water was pouring in.

The captain fumbled down the aft hatch to see if the bottom of the mast had been torn out of its socket. It was almost completely dark there; the lanterns had been extinguished when the storm first hit. He felt his way to the socket, sloshing through water knee-deep, half-stumbling over the ropes, hammocks, and galley gear that the storm had spilled across the planking. As far as he could tell, the socket was secure; if it had been pulled out, the ship would have sunk in minutes. The captain reached for a bunk along the bulkhead to guide himself back to the hatch, and touched something he did not expect.

At first he thought it must be a dead body, and he put his hand on the body's face to see if he would recognize one of his crewmen in the dark. But under his hand the face moved and a voice came.

"Why is it so dark?"

Jonah. The captain could hardly believe it. Why is it so dark? Had this fellow slept through the entire storm? While his crew was fighting for their lives, this jackal slept in his bunk?

"Get up!" the captain cried. "Get up and call on your god. Maybe he will listen to your voice, for none of the others have. Call on him, so that we will not die." The captain heard the panic begin to creep into his own voice. He dragged Jonah out of his bunk and into the knee-deep water. Then, jerking him by his cloak, the captain pulled him up onto the deck and dropped him there.

When the captain turned to his crew, he realized that he had lost them. While he had gone below, they had had nothing to do but panic. And now they stood stupidly on the deck, watching the waves pour over the ship,

holding on to the stump of the mast or the ropes tangled over the deck, screaming to their deaf gods, joining the chorus of the merchants.

"This is no ordinary storm," bellowed out one.

"The gods are angry with us," answered another.

"Not with us!" cried the first. "With someone on board!" Crewmen and merchants looked wildly around at each other.

"Lots!" called one of the merchants. "Let us choose lots to see who is responsible for this calamity!"

The crew looked to the captain, and he nodded his head. At least their fear had a focus now, he thought. Let them choose lots if it would make them more clearheaded.

The merchant who spoke produced the stones from a pouch tied to his side — a gamester, thought the captain. One by one the crew threw the stones across the heaving deck, and each time the stones showed innocence. Then the merchants threw their stones, and again they stood up innocent. And then the stones were handed to Jonah.

He hesitated a moment, then took the stones with something like regret. He threw them down to the deck and then, without waiting for them to stop rolling, held out his hands in guilt. It seemed as if the wind stilled for a moment, as if the waters quieted, as if heaven itself paused as the stones came to rest and indicated that this man, this man was responsible for the storm.

"Who are you?" cried the merchants.

The man looked down, his hands still out, his legs and feet struggling to steady him on the deck.

"I am a Hebrew. I worship the Lord of heaven, who made the earth and the seas. And I am running away from him."

The pause in the storm was over. The wind came, if possible, with even more fierceness, so that now the captain was truly afraid, feeling the rising panic. Jonah held onto a rope tied to the rail, watching the waves as they climbed over the ship.

"You there!" one of the crewmen screamed to Jonah. "Tell us how we may save our ship."

And Jonah said, his voice straining over the noise of the storm, "Throw me overboard!"

The crew and the merchants stood open-mouthed. The captain was sure that they had not heard him correctly. The wind must have grabbed his words and garbled them. "What did you say?"

"Throw me overboard!"

The man was clearly addled, stricken by fear, the captain thought. He would have to decide what to do — alone.

In desperation, he told his crew to man the oars. But their fierce rowing was no match for the fierceness of the storm. And just as he was about to issue another order, a wave struck the ship exactly in the middle at the moment it was climbing. It buried the prow in the oncoming mountain of water, filling the holds and sweeping away most of the rigging. After that, the captain could hardly believe they were still afloat.

"Captain!" It was the madman, Jonah. "Do as I say! Throw me overboard and the sea will calm."

It hardly mattered, thought the captain. You will be dead soon anyway. But he would not willingly drown a man from his ship and have that blood on his hands. Not when he was about to meet his own gods. The captain shook his head.

"Captain, would you kill each man here? I do not know what the God of heaven has in store for me, but I know that if I stay here, I will bring death to you all."

The captain looked out at his crew, their faces set in masks of terror so profound that he hardly recognized them. Then he made his decision.

"The Lord have mercy on us all for taking this life," he shouted. "Throw him over!"

No one stepped forward to do it — but then Jonah himself stepped to the first mate and clapped him on the shoulders. "Do as he says," he cried against the wind.

And so four of the crewmen, steadying themselves against the deck, picked Jonah up and hefted him out into the water.

At the last moment, the captain saw Jonah's eyes. There was no terror in them. And he looked not at the sea that would receive him, but at the sky.

And when he dropped beneath the angry foam, the storm stopped.

It wasn't like a storm that gradually died away, getting weaker and weaker until it finally disappeared into puffing breezes and misty air. It simply stopped. The clouds folded into themselves, the lightning ceased, the rain quit. Only a few remaining waves lifted the ship up and down, up and down.

Everyone aboard was stunned — and grateful. They made vows to Jonah's God. But no one said anything about Jonah.

The crew rigged a rudder and set a temporary mast in place. The seams below the deck closed back up — probably because the pitch and tar were still new and soft. Several men bailed out the holds and found the ship still to be in trim. For the rest of the journey, the winds blew steady and easy, heading into Tarshish.

Months later, the captain heard wild stories of a man swallowed by a great fish and spewed out on the banks of the Tigris, near Nineveh.

Jonah 1:1 – 2:10

Stories from the New Testament

Mary
AND THE ANGEL

ary was out gathering grapes in her father's vineyard when the air began to shimmer. At first she thought it was nothing — just the heat of the day and her feeling tired and all the excitement over her betrothal to the carpenter's son. But the shimmering brightened and brightened and then grew more solid until it all seemed to come together, and someone was standing there in the row beside the vines. It was an angel. She had never seen one before, but she knew it was an angel.

She did not know what to do. In all the stories she had heard, anyone who met an angel was supposed to fall face down on the earth, but she did not want to take her eyes away from what she saw. Perhaps she was supposed to run — but here she was with this enormous basket of grapes on her arm. And besides, she did not want to run. So she said the first words that came into her mind.

"Will you come into my house?"

At this the angel smiled gladly, and Mary knew it had been the right thing to say. The angel picked up one of the heavy baskets of grapes and followed her. Since she dared not take her eyes off the angel, she walked slowly backward until she stooped through the open doorway. With a start she wondered if the house would be big enough for God's angel. It was. He set the basket down on the wooden table beside a loaf of bread, then picked up a cluster of grapes and looked at it thoughtfully before putting it back. He turned to Mary.

"Mary, you are favored by God. The Lord is with you."

Mary did not know what the angel meant. She stood like a pillar, still holding the basket she had carried in. Gently the angel came to her — she feared him when he was so near, but she did not move — and took her basket, placing it on the table beside the first.

"Do not be afraid," he said. "You have found favor with God." But she could not help but be afraid. An angel had come to her! An angel was in her house!

The angel moved closer, and Mary wondered what the touch of an angel would be like. It must be as light as air and as burning as the sun. She sat down, her eyes still on the angel.

"Mary," he said, in a voice full of love, "you will have a child, a son, and his name shall be Jesus." Mary's eyes filled with surprise and fear, but he held up his hand to still her. "He will be great among all people. He will be called the Son of the Most High. The Lord will give him the throne of his father David, your ancestor. And he will reign over the house of Israel forever." The angel paused, and then smiled so joyfully that it hardly seemed as if the world could contain his merriment. "His kingdom will never end."

He stopped. It seemed as if Mary was expected to say something. But she could hardly speak. This could not be true. And yet it must be true, for there was the angel still standing in front of her, in her own house. Standing there as real as the basket of grapes he had carried in. Whatever would Joseph say to that?

Joseph! What would he say? Could he possibly believe her? And what would he say of the child to be born? A child.

Mary settled back into her chair, her thoughts so mixed that she wondered if she would ever be able to sort them out. Her awe of the angel, her love for Joseph, her fear, the image of a young child, the thought of her child as the son of the Most High — she closed her eyes.

"Do not be afraid," the angel repeated.

"But how can this be? I have never known a man. I cannot have a child."

"The Holy Spirit will come upon you," the angel explained. He held out his hands to her, palms upward. "The power of God will come upon you. And you will give birth to the Son of God." He smiled again, and with that smile Mary's fear began to give way, like the snow on the mountains melting into the brooks that bubbled down to bring life to the vineyards in the valley.

"And is it so impossible?" continued the angel. "Did not the Lord come upon Sarah when she was old and give her a son? And has not the Lord come upon Elizabeth, who wondered if she would ever bear a child?" Mary looked up, surprised, and the angel nodded. "Nothing is impossible with God," he said. And Mary knew that it was so.

She would have a child, and his name would be Jesus. He would be the son of the Most High, and he would reign over the house of Israel forever. Because nothing is impossible with God.

The sweet smell of the grapes was filling the room now, mixing with the yeasty smell of the bread baked earlier that morning. The fragrance of the bread and fruit, the wooden table, the broom in the corner, the low cot covered with a striped cloth — it was all so familiar. Yet now everything had changed. An angel had come to her house.

She bowed her head. "I am my Lord's servant. Let it be to me as you have said." When she looked up, the angel had gone, his blessing light upon her forehead.

There had been times in Mary's life when she had felt the Lord touch her, but she had never found the words to explain to anyone else what those touches had been like, what they had meant; she could only feel them in her memory. And so she had never spoken of them. But now words of joy and thankfulness came to her, singing through her mind. She knew what she would tell her cousin Elizabeth:

> *My soul praises the Lord*
> *and my spirit rejoices in God,*
> *For He has remembered His servant Mary.*
> *From now on, all generations will call me blessed*
> *because He has done great things for me.*
> *Holy is His name.*
> *He has kept His promise to Israel*
> *And brought mercy to the descendants of Abraham,*
> *Even as He said to our fathers.*

The light was starting to slant lower now, bringing in the dusk. Mary stood and looked out of her window, watching the lamps being lit throughout the village, lights against the darkness. She put her hand to her womb.

Beside her, the grapes glowed in the last red light of the sun.

Luke 1 : 2 6 - 5 5

Anna, Simeon,
AND THE BLESSING FULFILLED

It was one of those chilled, damp days when the cold sank deeply into Anna's bones. She sighed, wearily, and tried to think back. Had there been days like this when she was young? Had there been days like this when she had been married? She could remember none. Now, all days seemed chilled. She could never get warm.

She dressed and headed out toward the Temple. Cane in hand, she let her feet shuffle the dust into the air, even though it would mean washing her gown that night. She was too tired to lift her feet higher. The streets were crowded, and people brushed by her, hollering at donkeys, greeting friends, haggling over prices. She felt the annoyance of those who had come into the city early to find a good place to sell their goods; her shuffling was holding them back.

A n n a ,
S i m e o n ,
a n d   t h e
B l e s s i n g
F u l f i l l e d

—

103

She stood in a doorway to let them pass. So many people, moving so quickly, wanting to sell, wanting to buy, wanting to get to the Temple — like that family over there. They must have just arrived from the country, come to present their little one to the Lord. Anna smiled at the baby as they hustled past, and something stirred deeply inside her. She did not know what it meant.

But the Temple lay just ahead.

Here was one of the best moments of the day, when she first came near the Temple. She let herself be caught up in the noise, the sheer wonderful noise of it all. The beggars called, the merchants hawked their wares, doves cooed, white lambs bleated. The sound of prayers was going up from inside the Temple, and worshipers were milling about, turning their thoughts to God, forgetting one life to enter into another.

Anna hurried ahead. Soon she too would be at prayer, forgetting one life for another.

But once she was in the main courtyard, the chill was much worse. When her eighty-four-year-old eyes watered at the cold, the whole Temple blurred. Suddenly she felt very tired. Her last fast had left her weakened, and not only in her body. She had waited so long for something — she wasn't even sure what it was. Her husband had always told her that she was impatient, that she could not wait for the Lord to bring things about in his own time. Well, she had learned to be patient. She wished she could have shared the learning with him.

There were still times when she saw something, when she felt something, and her first thought was of telling it to him, sharing it with him. And then, so quickly that the two thoughts seemed one, she realized that he was gone, had been gone for a very long time. She would have told him about the family from the country, about the baby. But instead she decided she would tell what she felt to God, even though He knew all things already.

She had learned to wait.

Now her waiting was over.

Anna crossed the Temple courtyard, her feet cold on the cobbled stones, and entered the Court of the Women. She let her eyes travel up the spiraling pillars to the golden ceiling, dulled somewhat by the smoke of sacrifices, but still glowing like a Galilean sunset. The tapestries, the enameled floor, the rich, bejeweled robes of the priests swishing past — these belonged to another world, more real to Anna than the small house she had tended for so many lonely years. In fact, she was in the Temple so much that it seemed sometimes as if she never left it.

Resting one hand against a pillar — it too was so cold — she knelt slowly down and began to worship. The murmurs of the other women, the calls that came in from the other courts, even the sounds of her own whispered prayers died away, as they always did. She smiled, a smile so full of a stillness and peace that those who knew her only as that old widow would have been astonished to see how young she suddenly looked.

And then there came into her mind a picture so real, so vivid that she gripped her hand to her heart. It was the young family she had seen that morning.

She tried to push the picture away. She knew why she thought of them. She knew why her eyes welled with tears at the story of Sarah, and why the thought of that young baby in that busy street stirred a fire in her that she had hoped had long ago been snuffed out. She turned her mind back to God.

But the image would not go away. She seemed to see the family even more clearly now than she had in the street: the father, shouldering away the hawkers; the mother, covering her baby against the dust; the baby's head peeking out from the blanket, its hair washed with oil for the presentation. She could almost see them as they came toward the Temple. She pushed herself up with her cane and went outside.

*Anna,
Simeon,
and the
Blessing
Fulfilled*

—

105

She saw them immediately. She was somehow not surprised that she did. They were halfway up the Temple steps, and in front of them stood Simeon. Or was it Simeon? Anna was not sure. It had been many years since she had seen him standing so tall, so straight.

Anna watched as Simeon reached out his arms to the family. Usually they shook so badly that he could hardly eat; there was no tremor now. Anna wondered what the family would do, but there was no hesitation. The mother held out her child to Simeon, who took him and cradled him against his breast. And the baby did not cry.

But Simeon did. Great tears flowed down to his beard, and then onto the blanket that swaddled the baby. Simeon looked to heaven, and then back at the child in his arms. And then he spoke in a voice so strong that Anna was startled, and the noise of the Temple courts died away, and the people of Israel listened.

"Lord, as you promised, now dismiss me in peace." Simeon's eyes never left the baby. "My eyes have seen your salvation, the salvation that you have prepared as a blessing to the Gentiles, and for glory to your people Israel."

And suddenly Anna knew. She knew with a sureness unlike anything she had felt before. She knew now what had been stirring deep within her; it was not at all what she had thought. God had brought about this thing in his own time, and she was being called as a witness. For eighty-four years she had waited for this child. This is what she had been praying for, even without knowing it. Here was the blessing of the Lord.

Anna let the cane fall from her hand and walked toward the family.

Simeon handed the baby back to his parents, almost reluctantly. The mother took him, wrapped him up again, and laid her face against his with a soft smile.

With his hands lifted over them, Simeon spoke once more. "O Lord our God, our Lord who is One, bless this child as he blesses Your People." Then

Anna,
Simeon,
and the
Blessing
Fulfilled

—

107

he looked to the mother, and Anna, stepping closer, saw that once again his shoulders had started to stoop, his hands to tremble. "This child," he said to the mother, "will be a sword that will show the true hearts of many, and that will pierce your own soul as well." Simeon said the last words so quietly that only the mother, the baby, and Anna heard them.

Anna did not know what Simeon meant, but it did not matter to her. She did not see the hand that the baby's father laid on the mother's shoulder. She did not see the mother's eyes lift up to her. She saw only the baby. He lay cradled against his mother's chest, his eyes blinking and trying to focus, a bubble of spit on his lips. She reached out one hand to touch his soft head.

"He is the Lord's blessing," said the mother, with deep contentment in her voice.

Anna looked at her, nodding, hearing her own words come back to her. "I know this," she said. "He will be a blessing to us all, to all those who look forward to the redemption of Jerusalem. For all those who look for redemption."

"He is to be presented today," said the father now, filled with pride in his son. "Our first child."

Anna smiled and looked back at the baby. He seemed a bit bored with it all; his eyes were closing into sleep. "Present the child to the Lord, then," she said, and watched them climb the stairs, the father carrying two caged turtledoves, the mother holding tightly to the little one.

Anna sighed deeply, then hurried toward the Court of the Women. She forgot her cane, but there was no time to get it now. She had much to tell the women there, and then anyone else who came to worship.

Suddenly she felt very warm.

Luke 2:21-39

Peter AT THE
SHORE OF GENNESARET

Peter wondered if he had been able to hide the irritation in his face.

It was inconvenient, what this Teacher asked. And more than inconvenient. Hadn't he and James and John been out all night already? They had spent a long night on Lake Gennesaret — with no fish to show for their labor — and were in the middle of washing their nets, and here came this Teacher, asking to be rowed out a little from the shore so that he could teach the crowds gathered on the beach.

Peter yawned. If he had any guts, he would have said no. Let the man teach from the beach! He had better things to do than sit and listen to a Teacher. There were three holes in John's net to stitch up. And last night the brothers' boat (not his) had been taking on too much water — the lower seams needed a new coat of pitch. And then there were the fish to sell — well, not today, but almost every day. And then. . . . There were a hundred things that clamored at him. He yawned again. He wouldn't even mind going to sleep.

But this Teacher — he was not one to be refused. He really hadn't asked to use one of the boats at all; he had almost issued a command. "I have need of your boat," he had said, stepping into it. And that was all. Without a word (why hadn't he said anything?), Peter had left John and James, clambered into the boat, and rowed the Teacher a short ways from the beach. The words of the Teacher kept coming back to him: "I have need of your boat."

So he sat there as the heat of the morning pressed against the water, using the oars to keep the boat in place. Gennesaret was calm this hot day, and as Peter looked at the yellow sky he doubted whether the fishing would be good for the next twenty-four hours; all the fish would hide down at the bottom to escape the glare and the hot water on the surface. Every so often a small wave would tickle the boat's chin and run up on the shore, wetting the feet of the children gathered close. But mostly the water was still, as though it too were listening to the words of this Teacher. Peter laughed to himself — water stilling at the words of a man.

He wiped the moisture that had gathered beneath his eyes. The glare off the water had made them tear up.

Or were the tears because of what the Teacher said?

No. Peter was a fisherman, the best one on Gennesaret. Every day he and the brothers set out, watched by the other fishermen. Envied by the other fishermen. Peter had hands as wide and deep as shovels, arms that could drag in a net half-full of the silver fish that were so plentiful in Gennesaret, and hair red enough to announce his temper. There was no man he knew that he could not throw down, neither Jew nor — especially — Roman. And he did love to throw them down.

The Teacher was talking about the days of Jubilee now. But Peter wondered if he had ever walked into Jerusalem and seen the soldiers patroling the streets and desecrating the Temple. He wondered if he had seen the beggars maimed by Roman soldiers and the lepers abandoned by everyone. Or if he had walked outside the cities and seen the hills where the Romans did their crucifying. Days of Jubilee indeed. The tears gathered in his eyes.

When the Messiah came, Peter thought, he would stand with him, sword in hand. Then there would be such a Jubilee as this land of the Lord's had never seen. There would be such a bloodletting that all of Gennesaret could not cleanse it. Peter gripped the oars tightly, as though they were javelins, and imagined what it would be like to feel the life of a Roman ebb away between his hands.

And then the Teacher finished speaking. He sat down in the boat, tired. Peter waited for the crowd to draw back so that he could row the boat ashore and let the Teacher off. But the crowd did not draw back. They called his name into the wind: "Jesus." The children looked at him, laughing. The men and women looked at him, filled with longing. And the old ones, helped to their feet by children and grandchildren, wept openly, as though they had come upon something they had waited for all of their lives.

The Teacher had his back to Peter, and Peter wondered what Jesus' eyes would be like now. And then he knew, because Jesus turned around and looked at him, looked into him.

Peter turned to stone. The eyes were full of . . . jubilee. But they were full of pain too. This Teacher had seen the beggars and the lepers and the crucifixion hills outside the cities. And still his eyes were full of jubilee. He eased his hold on the oars and waited for the Teacher to say something.

He waited a long time. The crowd on the beach finally began to move off. The boat lay still, though Peter could feel a breeze freshen against his back. Tears still collected in the creases of skin under his eyes, and Peter forgot to wipe them away. For a long time, he and Jesus looked at each other, and still Peter waited for him to say something. When he finally did, it was not what Peter had expected.

"Put out into deep water. Let down the net for a catch."

Peter stared at him, astonished. What did this man know of fishing? He might be a Teacher, but Peter was the fisherman. He hesitated. "Master, we worked hard all night, and we caught nothing."

Jesus put up his hand to stop Peter's objections. "Put out into deep water. Let down the net for a catch," he repeated.

Peter sighed. All night they had caught nothing. All night. And now, in the heat of the day, the fish would be at the bottom, hidden, beyond the casts of nets. But just as before, he knew the Teacher was not really asking him to do this. "Master," Peter said, "because you say so, I will let down the net."

Peter gripped the oars tightly and began to row out, the rhythm of the rowing feeling good against the tight muscles of his back. The breeze had grown, and far off on the lake he could see small whitecaps, ripples pretending to be waves. He smiled. There was something about being on the water that made him happy. He looked over at Jesus and was half-surprised to find him smiling too, taking pleasure in the waves and the cool air that had pushed aside the heat.

About a third of the way out, still in sight of the shore, Jesus signaled for Peter to stop. Peter shook his head. If they got further out, there might be a chance. But his fisherman's sense told him there would be no fish here. The water was too shallow, and the earlier heat would have driven the fish to the bottom. But Jesus insisted. So Peter let the boat drift still and then, together with Jesus, he let the net out, hand over hand, into the water.

The net began to grow heavy even before it was fully let out. Peter felt his forearms stiffen against the weight. The net must be snagged on the bottom somehow. He drew it along the side of the boat to release it, and then felt the net jerk from his hands.

He looked at Jesus, who was still holding the net, jubilee laughter in his eyes.

Frantically Peter stood up and waved to the shore. James and John, who had been watching, wondered what Peter was doing out on the lake with the Teacher when there weren't any fish. Still, they dragged their boat (slow leaks and all) into the water. When they reached Peter and the Teacher, Peter had found his hold on the net and was tying off hundreds and hundreds of fish. Together the four men grabbed hold of the two sides of the net and heaved it to the surface, spilling the silver catch into the boats, spilling and spilling and spilling it until the fish began to slide off the heaps and back into the lake. And still the jubilee laughter crackled from Jesus' eyes.

And suddenly Peter knew what the old ones on the beach had already known, and perhaps what the children had known as well. He loosed his hold on the straining net, bowed down, and wept. "Lord," he said, "I am a sinful man. You should not be with me."

Jesus took Peter's hands — hands that would never hold the javelins Peter had hoped for — and put them back on the net. "Do not be afraid," Jesus said. Together they finished hauling in the catch and then set out for the beach, the decks almost level with the lakewater, fish jumping and sliding and leaping up into the air, their bodies arched in the bright sun and cool breeze. When the boats reached the shore, Jesus helped the three men with the net, and Peter worked beside him, gathering in the fish.

When the work was finished, Jesus turned to Peter. He had tied his robe below his waist — just like the fishermen did — and it was dripping water. His hair was wet too, and scales from the fish sparkled up and down his forearms. He put a hand on Peter's shoulder, a hand heavy with the smell of the life they had together brought out of the lake.

"From now on you will catch men."

Peter, James, and John pulled the boats up on the beach. Leaving everything behind, they followed Jesus up the road toward the beggars and lepers that Jesus and Peter had seen. And to a hill outside of a city.

Luke 5:1-11

The Samaritan Woman AT THE WELL

It was one of those hot, scorching mornings when she knew that she would be glad just to make it through the day. She gathered her dark robes around herself, feeling the grit of the sand in them, and sighed. The early dawn was past, and already the other women would be at the well. She would have to wait, and by the time she got there, the water would be low and clouded with dirt.

Well, it was her lot. It was only what she deserved, she thought.

So she waited in the dark heat of her house as the morning dragged the dusty sun higher into the sky and the women of the town met over the well, chatting of the day's news and herding goats and sheep and children before them. She could see it all in her mind: the laughing and the happy calls, the bleating and baaing. After they drew the water they needed, the women would sit together and begin sifting the wheatheads and . . .

No. She would not let herself think of these things. She was alone now and forever. That was all there was to it. She was completely alone.

She stood up and went into the storeroom, feeling in the darkness for the clay jar she would use to carry the water. It was so dry against her hands that she could imagine it falling into dust and blowing away into the desert, its shape and its use forgotten.

But this is not what would happen to her. She would not blow away. What she was, she was, and if she was no longer part of the village, still she was herself, a Samaritan woman. And perhaps somehow, some day, things would get better. Holding the jar under one arm, she stooped to pick up the bucket by the threshold of her home and cradled it in the crook of her other arm. Then, touching the mezuzah and kissing her fingertips without thought, she passed outside and blinked her eyes against the too-bright light.

"There she is!" called a young voice from down an alley.

So it had started so soon. She couldn't even get to the square without the voices like stones thudding against her back. She went on, her face covered by the dark robes.

She tried not to see the faces of those who looked at her like she was something filthy that could stain them just by being close. She tried not to hear the silence that shouted at her when she passed groups of women that she had once known. She thought only about the dust that the hem of her robes spread into the heated air, and the tread of her feet toward the dirtied well.

If there was no one at the well today when she got there, perhaps she would be spared the humiliation of standing like a pillar of salt under the sun, waiting in the heat until the very last person had finished. Waiting alone while everyone in the courtyard looked at her and thought the same thing.

When she turned the last corner and passed by the last silent group, she took her eyes from the ground to look at the well, and her heart slowed. There was someone still there. She stopped and looked down again, holding her robes close to her to shield her from . . . many things. She listened for the strain of the rope against the pulley, the clunking of the filled bucket on the stone sides of the well. Then she would know that she could look up again and get her own water.

The sounds did not come. She looked up anyway.

He had not moved. And with a start, she realized how strange it was that a man should be there at this time in the morning. She lowered her eyes, and then looked again. Still he had not moved. It seemed to her as if he could not be moved, and that she must go to the well even though he would be there.

She went, feeling him look at her, not as other men had looked at her, but as if he knew more about her than she knew herself.

She was puzzled as she drew closer and he still did not move. He was a Jew; she could see that now. A Jew in this Samaritan town. She was surprised he would dare to come here, where everyone hated him for what he was. Well, perhaps she wasn't so surprised; she herself knew the feeling.

She stopped on the far side of the well from the man, not looking at him. She set the clay pot on the ground, tied the wooden bucket to the rope that hung over the well, and began to let the rope slide wet through her fingers. Then, when she felt the bucket slosh into the water and grow heavy against her arms, she hauled it up, hand over hand. When the bucket reached the top of the well, she pulled it toward her and began to empty the water — quite clear today — into the clay jar.

"Will you give me a drink?"

She looked up and into the eyes of the man. He had spoken to her! A Jew had spoken to a Samaritan?

Suddenly she grew angry. Perhaps he was no different from the others. Perhaps he knew what everyone thought she was.

"You are a Jew," she spat. "Do you not see I am a Samaritan woman?

How can you ask me for a drink?" It was as if she was spitting at all the silent people who had watched her, who had judged her. She felt the anger grow strong in her, and tried desperately not to let the hurt deep within her burst out — and not to let the tears show.

The man took a long time answering, and she found herself waiting for him, hardly knowing why, hoping that something would happen.

His voice came back so gently that her tears could not help but come. It sounded like a voice that she had longed for all of her life, without really knowing that she had longed for it.

"Woman, if you knew the gift of God that is before you, and who it is that is asking you for a drink, you would have understood that he is not offering judgment." She looked at him, startled. "You would have asked him, and he would have given you living water."

Suddenly there was nothing else in the world except for this man and her. Nothing else. All her life had led to this single moment, this meeting with a stranger by the well. The death and anger and sorrow and frustration in her life — they had all led to this, and she knew that what she would say next was terribly, terribly important.

She handed him the clay jar, and he took it and upended it easily, so that the water came bright against his cheeks.

"Sir," she asked slowly, "where can you get this living water? You have nothing to draw with, and the well is deep."

The man put down the jar. He nodded, still smiling, and did not answer.

"Are you greater than our father Jacob, who gave us this well and drank from it himself?"

The man spread his arms wide, as though to explain — or perhaps bless. "How often do you come to this well?"

"Every morning."

"Why?"

"Because I am thirsty when the new day comes." Her anger had left her now, but she was still puzzled. Of course she must come every day to this well. How else could she live?

"Everyone who drinks water from this well is soon thirsty again. But the water I give is not like that." He handed the clay jar back to her, empty. "Whoever drinks the water I give will never be thirsty again." He leaned forward. He was not smiling now. He was looking at her clearly and deeply, and she felt as if he were looking right through her skin the way someone would look through water, clearing aside the muck to find the true bottom. "The water I give will become a spring of water, welling up into eternal life."

Could it be so? she wondered. Could it truly be so?

She felt within her something she had never felt before. Somehow, everything was suddenly possible. But she could hardly dare to hope. So she asked a question to stall, a question whose answer she already knew.

"Sir, can you give me this water so that I will never again have to come to this well?"

The man looked at her, half-smiling, but with sadness in his eyes, as if he knew all the pain she felt, all the humiliation she went through day after hot day. So he did not answer her question, but looked for something deeper.

"Go," he said, "and call your husband. Bring him here to me."

The woman was startled. Had he heard something in the square, some gossip? But no. No Samaritan would ever talk to a Jew. He knew somehow without her telling.

"I have no husband," she said, turning back to lower the bucket again into the well.

"What you say is true," he answered. "But not completely true."

She nodded. The stranger was right. It was not completely true at all. And there was only one way that he could know this. "You are a prophet who sees," she said. "My people have had prophets as well, who have led us to worship on the Samarian mountains. But we are different from you Jews. You say that we must worship only in Jerusalem."

A look of pain crossed the stranger's face. "Are we so very different?" he asked. "Believe me when I tell you this: a time is coming when you and I will not worship in Samaria's mountains or in Jerusalem alone. God is not in one place or another, but in all places. He is Spirit, and He is Truth. And those who worship Him must worship Him in spirit and in truth."

And there it was, as simple as drawing water, as powerful as a never-ending spring welling up in the desert of her soul. It did not matter that he was a Jew and she a Samaritan. It did not matter that he was a man and she a woman. It did not matter if she climbed the mountains or journeyed to Jerusalem. God looked for worshipers who worshiped and loved Him in spirit and in truth.

Suddenly she was no longer thirsty, and as she looked at the man, she knew that he was more than a prophet.

"I know that the Messiah is coming some day. When he comes" — she paused, as if daring to hope — "when he comes, he will explain all this to us."

The man stood and went to the well. He drew the bucket up and poured the water into her clay jar. Handing it to her, he told her what he had never told anyone else. He told her the good news that would lead to the salvation of this woman and many in the town that she would bring to him. He told her what she had dared to hope.

"I am the Messiah."

John 4:4-26

Jesus
AND THE PARALYZED MAN

*I*t's only what you should expect," said his neighbor.
"When you invite a man like Jesus into your house, you're asking for all sorts of trouble."

The owner of the house nodded, not listening. He was looking up at the ceiling.

"Look at the people who gather around him. Oh, some are all right, like those Pharisees from Jerusalem standing over there, but most aren't. Just smell them!"

The owner nodded again and tried to move away, but his neighbor grabbed him by the elbow.

"And you know, they say that he eats with tax collectors and . . . well, even worse than those. He's not the sort I'd invite into my house."

The owner nodded one more time, wondering how he was going to clear a space in front of Jesus.

"And now this," said the neighbor, pointing to the ceiling.

The man pulled his arm away and looked at his neighbor questioningly, as though he was looking at him for the very first time. "Don't you see what's happening here?"

"I see that your roof is being torn apart. You had better hope it doesn't rain."

A shaft of sunlight now poked through a hole in the ceiling, paused, and then leapt down to the feet of Jesus, where it spread into a warm pool. The man smiled. It looked like the pool of Siloam, its waters rippling around Jesus' feet.

Carefully, so that nothing would fall on the heads of those crowded into the house, four men were making a hole in the roof, pulling away pieces of the thatch of dried mud, straw, and branches. The owner of the house was surprised that all he was doing was watching from below. At any other time he would have rushed upstairs to stop them. He had worked long hours under a Galilee sun to secure the thatch against the rafters, making it dense enough so that it pattered the rain away. Now, if he could have squeezed his way out of the crowd and through the door, he would have helped them rip out the thatch. But then, nothing was the same today.

Jesus had stopped speaking. He was watching too, as if he knew what was coming. In fact, all the crowd now looked up at the blue sky stretching itself wider and wider through the ceiling. Suddenly the sifting down of the occasional piece of straw stopped, and the man heard the soft sounds of feet shuffling around on the rooftop. And then the hole was filled with stretched linen, blocking out everything but glints from the sun around the edges.

Once it cleared the ceiling, he could tell right away what it was: the kind of mat the beggars used all up and down the roads of Capernaum, a single square of cloth that marked out everything they owned in all the world. The four ends of this mat were bunched up and tied, and he could hear the scraping of the ropes against the thatch at the edges of the hole as four men — there must have been four to keep the mat so level — lowered it down out of the sky into the pool of sunlight at Jesus' feet.

It was not a long way to the floor, but the men lowered so slowly, so carefully that it took some time for the mat to finally touch the ground, the four corners to relax, and the ropes to slacken. Immediately, four faces peered down through the hole.

"Look who it is," the neighbor cried, disgusted. "Right in your own house! On your own floor!" The owner hushed him. People stood around the man on the floor in a tight circle; they didn't have much choice, since there were so many of them crowded into so small a space. Those behind strained to look over the heads of those in front. "Who is it? Who is it?" called those who couldn't see. And the word went back: "The paralyzed beggar."

There were some groans of disappointment in reply. It was only the beggar that they had seen all their lives, his two unformed legs, skin at the bones, tight up beneath him. The Pharisees held linen cloths sweetly scented with delicate oils up to their faces.

The crowd quieted, waiting to see what Jesus would do. The beggar said nothing. The owner of the house held his breath. It seemed as if he was on the very edge of something extraordinary. He felt his heart beating against his tightened chest.

Jesus seemed suddenly unaware of the crowd. He looked down at the beggar, who had never walked one step. He looked up at the four faces peering down through the hole. Then his eyes filled with tears, and he shook his head and smiled. He looked back to the paralyzed man and laid his hand on the man's head; the sunlight that had pooled at his feet now sprinkled between his fingers.

"Your friends are men of great faith," he said.

The crippled man nodded.

The house owner edged closer; even his neighbor was quiet now. Could it be that Jesus would run his hand down the cripple's legs and straighten them? Would Jesus perform one of his healing miracles right here in this house? His chest grew tighter. Was this what he was on the edge of?

And then he found that it was not. He was on the edge of a miracle even more wonderful.

Jesus looked up once more at the four faces, and then turned back to the man on the mat. "Friend," he said quietly, his hand still on the man's head, "your sins are forgiven."

The owner of the house did not hear the explosion of outrage from the Pharisees in the corner, or the murmuring disappointment from the crowd that had wanted something spectacular. He was watching the face of the crippled man, and what he saw there was what he had watched and waited for all his life. This Jesus had done what only God could do. The man knew it as surely as he knew he was in his own house. Jesus had performed the greatest miracle of all. He had forgiven.

But the Pharisees grew louder, and the crowd looked at them anxiously. They turned to each other, gesturing at Jesus and the beggar.

The crippled man, the four men peering down from the roof, and the owner of the house looked only at Jesus.

Now the Pharisees were shouting. "This man blasphemes! Who is he to forgive sins? This is a matter to be brought before the Council!"

One left, shouldering his way through the crowd importantly. The others glared at Jesus, who had not stopped looking into the soul of the crippled man. Finally Jesus, as if he felt their glares knifing into his back, turned and looked at them. And when he spoke, there was anger in his voice.

"Why do you reason back and forth this way? Why do you puff up your hearts against the Lord? Tell me, those of you skilled in the law, which is easier to say: 'Your sins are forgiven' or 'Rise and walk'?"

The Pharisees raised their eyebrows and looked away. They did not choose to answer.

Jesus turned his eyes back to the crippled man. "Friend," he said loudly, "so that you may know that I have the authority to forgive your sins, I say this to you: Stand, fold your mat, and return home."

There was almost no time between the moment when Jesus spoke and the moment when the man was standing on legs that looked as strong as if he had run upon them without tiring all his life. At once there were calls of joy from the four men on the rooftop, and then they disappeared; the house owner could imagine them leaping from the roof to the stairs to the front of the house to meet their friend. There were gasps from the crowd, angry cries from the Pharisees, and, from the cripple, a song of praise, one of David's, that others took up and sang as the crowd emptied into the street, following the man forgiven and healed as he walked for the first time to his house.

Soon, only Jesus and the owner remained behind. Jesus thanked him for the use of his house and offered to help rethatch the roof. He had done it many times in Nazareth. He declined a bed for the night; he would travel out into the countryside that evening. The owner of the house could offer him only one thing more, Jesus said.

The owner knew what it was. He knelt at Jesus' feet, home for the first time. Then, quietly, when no one else was there to see, Jesus performed the greater miracle — again.

Mark 2 : 1 - 12

THE TENTH
Leper

On the border between Galilee and Samaria, in a place that was part of neither country, ten men lived away from everyone else. They huddled in hill caves that were as dry and hot as kilns. They never went to the shores of any of the nearby lakes. They never went to the marketplace. They never went to the Temple. They never did anything but slowly die.

They were lepers. No one ever came near them. Their families would leave food and water in a small hut near the caves, but they never stayed to watch the lepers come to collect the supplies. The sight of them was too terrible. And, to tell the truth, the lepers did not want to be seen. Who would want their families to see the oozing sores and dry scales that made hideous patchworks of their bodies? They knew that in the towns where they had come from, no one spoke of them anymore.

They buried their dead themselves. Nine of the men were all but dead already. They watched the wounds on their bodies weep away their life, and they sat in the shadows, waiting for sleep and more than sleep. They did not fear dying as much as they feared living.

But one man was not ready to die. He held on to life through his fierce anger. Each night before he slept and each day when he awoke, he cursed the world he lived in, wishing that he could blight it as the world had blighted him.

He thought of the family that was afraid to see him. "Thanks to you," he snarled under his breath, "I am alone."

He thought of how he had gotten this awful disease. He remembered the beggar that he had found, apparently asleep, on the road to Samaria, how he had gone to waken him so that he would not be run over by the carts of merchants lumbering along, and how, when he had turned the beggar over, he had found that the man was not asleep, but dead. Only two weeks later the leprosy that had killed the beggar set a sore festering on the back of his hand. "Thanks to you," he raged, "I am here."

He thought of the priests, fat and sleek in their temple robes. "Thanks to you," he muttered to himself, "I am not allowed to approach God."

And when he thought of God, he thought of One who had made him into this unclean thing that everyone feared, that everyone shunned. Whenever he came near to others, dogs barked and boys threw stones. Even if he shouted out his shame before him — "Unclean! Unclean!" — he could not avoid their hate. This is what God had brought him to. "Thanks to you," he said between clenched teeth, one more time. "Thanks to you."

Sometimes he would climb out from the caves and watch the road that leaned its dusty way against the hills. One way led to Galilee; the other way led to Samaria — and home. Sometimes he would climb down to the road just to see if any of his old neighbors would pass that way. Once he had recognized a neighbor whose field he had helped to plow every springtime. Their children had played with each other in the furrows. But when he had called out, waving (his long-sleeved garment hid the sores on his arms), the neighbor had looked away from his voice. The leper had never called out again.

On this day he was lonely. His family had forgotten to bring him his supplies; this had happened more and more often over the past few weeks. He climbed away from the caves, the salt of his tears stinging the sores open on his cheeks. The air was so sickly yellow in the caves that even the other near-dead men climbed after him to see if they might catch a breeze up higher. When the leper looked behind him and saw the other nine, he was suddenly glad, though he quickly let his anger swallow his gladness.

They lay there for the better part of the morning, ten dying lepers, watching the world go by on the road from Galilee to Samaria, and no one ever looked up at them.

Toward noon, when the sun burned overhead, a group heading toward Galilee stopped below the hill and settled themselves in a patch of shade. The leper was puzzled; no one ever stopped in this spot. Everyone knew that this was near the caves where the lepers lived. He lifted his body and leaned forward. Such a strange thing, he thought, and strained to hear the conversation.

"We are going up to Jerusalem," he heard one of the men say. "And there, everything that was written about me by the prophets will be fulfilled. On the third day, the Son of Man will rise again."

"But Jesus, we do not understand what this means." This from a large, burly fellow with red hair and big hands.

The man spread his hands as if to explain, but the leper did not hear the reply. He realized that the man was Jesus — the same Jesus he had heard about before he had gotten leprosy. It was said — oh, Lord! — it was said that he had the power of God in him to heal.

"Up!" he cried to the nine others. "Up! This is Jesus of Nazareth. Up, for the love of God!"

The nine raised their heads slowly, as though the sun were pushing them down into the rocky ground. The tenth leper helped them to their feet — their scaling, oozing feet — and set them moving down the hillside toward the road. One could no longer move, and the tenth leper, in near desperation, hefted him onto his back and staggered down the hill, crying, "Jesus, Master, have pity on us!" The others joined him in his plea. The thin cries of the ten lepers seemed to sicken the air around them. Everyone in the group down on the road stood — except for Jesus. They rushed in front of him, these disciples, and the one with the red hair stepped before them all, one of his large hands resting on a sword.

But the lepers continued down the hill.

"Jesus, have mercy upon us! Jesus!"

The first eight lepers stopped on the far side of the road, held back by the furrowed brow of the red-haired man. The tenth leper struggled down to the bottom of the hill, carrying his near-dead load, gasping for breath in the heat. He could no longer call out. He fell by the road and lay beneath his burden.

Now Jesus stood and passed through his disciples, the air softening around him.

The leper could not look up. The heat and the dust and the quiet were all one. He could not croak out even one more call for pity.

Then a shadow, cool and calm, moved over him, over them all. And then the shadow was Jesus' voice.

"Go," he said, and it was as if his voice raised them from the dead. "Go show yourselves to the priests in the Temple." The cool breeze that sprang up came under the leper's chest and lifted him first to his knees, then to his feet. It revived the man he had been carrying too — so much so that he sprang up

and joined the others. When the tenth leper raised his eyes, Jesus had already disappeared behind his disciples and was sitting down again. On the road toward Galilee, the nine lepers were hobbling — or were they running? — toward the town, eager to find the priests.

The tenth leper stood strong against the sunlight, and then turned and ran, faster and faster, feeling the wind dry his sores, feeling the dry scales fall away from his skin, feeling . . . Lord, just feeling! He ran on, though he could not catch the others, who were leaping and jumping like young lambs toward town. He felt like the young boy he had once been, running up and down the Samarian hills, never tiring. Like an eagle riding the rolling air beneath him.

Even so, he was afraid to look down. He had heard of things like this — a man caught in delirium, imagining he was doing things he could not do. Perhaps he still lay on the crest of the hill, broiling in the sun, and none of this had happened. Perhaps . . .

He looked down, and desperately, achingly, he held his hands up before his face, felt his cheeks, felt his arms and legs and feet. And he knew then that he was healed. He stopped in the middle of the road and held his hands up toward the sky, pushing the sunlight back. The shouts and wild cries of the nine ahead of him grew faint in the distance.

The leper turned back, away from the town and the priests, back to Jesus. He found Jesus coming down the road toward him, the disciples still around him. They parted now at his coming, and the leper saw Jesus raising his hands to him, and suddenly he was at Jesus' feet, sobbing over and over, "Thanks to you. Thanks to you."

Luke 17:11-19

The Centurion at Calvary

It was, as far as the weather went, a most unusual day.

Everything else was the same as it had been for day after day after day, for week after week after week. For the centurion, it had all been business as usual. There had been some sort of near riot in the city the night before — nothing unusual there. There had been a trial and a man condemned to be crucified — nothing unusual there. He was said to have been some kind of rebel — as if a Jew in this God-forsaken land could hope to stir up any real rebellion against imperial Rome.

But the weather was certainly unusual. At noon it grew dark.

The centurion looked around him. There was the Cyrene that he had plucked from the crowd to carry the rebel's cross. Usually he let the condemned man carry it himself all the way out of the city and up to the Hill of the Skull. But Pilate must have been harsh with this one. He had fallen three times before the centurion had seen the broad back of the Cyrene and had made him carry the rebel's burden.

Over there was a group of women. Not unusual. There was often a mother or a wife or a sister, crying. The centurion was accustomed to that and no longer moved by it. Most of these were crying, except for one old woman, who was holding her hands to her heart. At least, he didn't think she was crying; it was getting harder and harder to see in this darkness.

Not far from the women, a group of his own men leaned against their spears, watching those gambling over what the condemned had owned. The men were bored; they had done this a hundred times, and it was a messy duty that didn't really make them feel like soldiers. They would all rather go off into the hills and do some real fighting than nail a man to a board. The centurion flexed his hands and looked again at the dark sky.

Laughter rippled across the hill, high-pitched laughter. At first the centurion thought it might be from one of the three dying men. Sometimes they went like that, mad just before the end. But it wasn't from the men at all. The laughter was coming from a group of Jews who had come up from the city to watch the rebel die. That wasn't unusual, either: Often the family of a victim would come to insult the dying murderer. Sometimes the centurion had even had to separate the mother of a murdered man and the mother of the murderer. That was no business for a centurion of Rome. But the ones today — they were different. These were the chief priests of the city; he wondered why they were so interested in seeing the rebel die.

Was that a tremor he felt in the earth beneath him? No. No one else seemed to have noticed.

The thief on the left cross was spitting at the group of Jews, and the centurion smiled to see them back away so that they would not have their fine robes soiled on this hill of blood. Having finished with the Jews, the thief turned to the soldiers, still gambling over a robe. The wind was coming up and carried the words away from him, but the centurion knew what they must have been. It often went like this. First they would beg for death. And then, as the pain of the cross grew unbearable, they would shout insults to goad the soldiers into killing them quickly. He himself had fallen for this trick when he had first arrived in Palestine, and as punishment his centurion had made him stand watch for three days and nights. The soldiers had all become so used to the pattern that they didn't bother to reply.

The thief on the left turned now to the rebel. His face was twisted horribly in his hate and pain, and his eyes popped wildly. "You called yourself the King of the Jews. Now's the time for one of your miracles if there ever was one. Save yourself and us, if you can. Are you the Messiah or not?"

The centurion listened for his answer. There was none. The man's head hung low, blood dripping down his face from the crown of thorns that dug into his head — the joke of some of his soldiers.

Suddenly the thief on the right, who had not spoken until this time, called to the thief across from him. "Don't you fear God? We die for what we have done, but this man has done nothing."

The centurion was startled. Never before had he heard anything like this coming from one being executed.

The man was breathing heavily, as if speaking had exhausted him. But he roused himself and looked toward the rebel. "Lord," he paused to get his breath, "remember me when you come into your kingdom."

The rebel raised his head, heavy with blood. His arms, though racked out on the cross, seemed to be stretching out to embrace the man beside him. His lips, black and cracked, opened, but the voice that came out was not that of a dying man but of . . . The centurion was not sure what.

"I tell you what is true: This very day you will be with me in that kingdom."

The Jews gathered nearby laughed and sneered. Even some of his own men snickered, the centurion noticed. "You will be with me in that kingdom." This was a madness he had not heard before.

The centurion cleared his throat and spat. He counted again the weeks until his duty in Palestine would be over. He hoped that the gods — and the emperor — would see fit to find a better station for him. Perhaps Sicily for a time, with the olive-skinned women, then up north to Germany for some real fighting. And after that, perhaps a tour in Gaul, where there was glory to be had.

What could the rebel have meant about a kingdom?

Certainly what he felt then was a tremor. Even the others seemed to have felt it. The Jews gathered their robes around them and began hurrying back to the city. They had seen enough, he supposed. The soldiers — who had finished their gambling — stood up and looked at the ground uneasily, as if they could somehow peer into it and see what had shaken them.

And the old woman only looked deeper into her own heart.

Suddenly the rebel raised his head, and as the wind stilled for a moment he cried to the open sky, "Eli, Eli, lama sabachthani." Then his head dropped.

The centurion looked around. Behind him he saw the Cyrene and caught his eye. So he too had stayed to see the end of this.

"What did that man just say?" the centurion demanded.

The Cyrene looked at him fixedly — an unusual thing for a Cyrene to do to a Roman, especially a centurion. "He cried out to God," he answered. "He asked God why He had abandoned him."

Suddenly the man gave one more great cry, and the centurion spun around in time to see his muscles sag into death.

Now the darkness pressed down like a heavy hand. Frightened, people rushed down the hill toward the city gates. The centurion's soldiers broke the legs of the two thieves; they would die now within a few minutes. The body of the man in the center hardly needed the test that his men gave to it. The centurion had seen death enough to recognize it.

The earth trembled again, and the centurion put out his spear to balance himself. Beneath the cross, he saw the old woman — probably the man's mother — standing. She stood quite still, as though the earth were not reeling under her.

The darkness grew even thicker, pressing down against the shoulders of the rebel. And suddenly the centurion knew that if it were not for the shoulders of that dead man, he would be crushed. The darkness would fall upon him like stones. Because he too felt that God had abandoned him.

Then the trembling of the earth stopped, and like sweet honey the words of the dead thief came into his mind: "Lord, remember me." And the rebel had promised that he would.

The centurion stood up. How had he come to fall upon the ground? This was no ordinary day. This was no ordinary man. Surely, he thought, surely this is the Son of God. And somehow the centurion knew just as surely that he would be remembered, as though he had somehow, for some reason, received a blessing he could never have anticipated.

The centurion called his soldiers together and started them down the hill. He followed slowly behind them, his arms folded across his chest, his hands reaching up and clutching his shoulders.

Matthew 27:32-54
Luke 23:26-47

In the Garden

The garden was as quiet that morning as if Adam and Eve had just walked out of it and left it empty forever. All the night creatures had finished making their noises and had found some dark place to sleep through the hot hours. But dawn's pink lingered in the sky, so the birds still had their heads tucked under their wings, heaving their quick little breasts to take in the air still cool from the night.

Joseph had chosen the garden because it was so quiet. On one side the living rock rose out of the earth, its top smoothed by the sand blown against it every day of the year. But below that, the rock guarded an acre of olive trees, glossy green now in the springtime, their trunks old but straight, their roots stretching down deeper than anyone could imagine to find water. It was the kind of place that Joseph liked to visit so that he could read quietly, alone. He wanted to be buried there.

But the garden had been busier two days ago.

The wind and storm of that day had rustled even this place, tearing off the new leaves on the olive trees and sending them skimming up the rock and out into the dark noontime. And then later, in that strange green calm, a small group had come, their tears flowing without sound, carrying a body wrapped in anointed linen. Joseph himself had helped to push away the stone across the tomb that he had cut into the rock, and he had led the way in, carrying a lamp and setting it in a socket hung on the rock, where it would burn dully for a few days. Two men had carried the body in, followed by two women. They had set it on the rock slab as gently as if it had been only asleep, not minding the blood that was seeping through the linen onto the stone, like a lamb's blood on an altar.

One of the women had carried a sack, and from it the others had drawn more pieces of linen, wrapping them again and again around the body, now stiffening in the late afternoon heat. Then, finished, they had stood back, as if not sure what to do next. They could not look at each other. Slowly they had moved outside the tomb, and, with Joseph, rolled the stone across the entrance. They had stood outside a long time, waiting for something to happen, not wanting to leave because it would mean an ending.

The following day the Roman soldiers had come to secure the tomb. The chief priests and the Pharisees had gone to Pilate, worried that the drama with the man who had called himself the King of the Jews wasn't over. "Sir," they said, "we remember how that imposter said, while he was still alive, 'After three days I will rise again.'" So Pilate had instructed them to send the soldiers to take care of things. The soldiers sealed the tomb with the red wax seal of the governor. And they put guards on watch to see that the dead man did not escape.

By the third day, life in the city had gone back to normal, it seemed. And the garden had grown quiet again, too. The seal of the stone had not been disturbed, and now the soldiers, leaning against their spears and pulling their long cloaks around them against the dampness, were waiting for the sun to come up and warm them. A long night, watching by a grave.

It was the birds that called out to the coming dawn. Such a chorus of them, singing and chirping and clucking and snapping their calls as if there were something different about this morning. When the soldiers looked up into the trees, they were surprised at the robins that had gathered there, their red breasts looking gray in the sleepy light. The soldiers stamped their feet; their shoulders shivered in the last cold of the night.

Through the olive trees at the east end of the garden, they watched the light stretch up into the sky, slowly, slowly, like the sun was waiting for just the right moment to step out and make its patrol. The horizon grew brighter and brighter, and the light chimed against the clouds — and then there was the sun, white hot against the dark earth, striking the shivering cold as if it were the enemy to be overcome.

The light dazzled across the land, broke through the olive trees, and hit the stone face on. And as the soldiers watched — their knees loosened, their faces tight with fear, the iron javelins fallen from their hands — the stone rolled away. The light, which seemed almost like a presence, pushed into the open tomb and was met by — could this be? — an even stronger light bursting from inside, so that the two met in a cloud of brilliant white, too bright to look upon.

Nothing like it had been seen in a garden for a very, very long time.

By the time the light had faded, the soldiers had gone. They scurried away on their hands and knees, eyes shut, groping for a way out of the garden. They found it easily enough and pelted through the streets of Jerusalem to report to the governor's palace. On their way, they passed three women carrying jars of ointment, out early this morning.

But in the garden, everything was quiet again. The birds were going about their business for the day; there were all the young to feed. The olive trees were stretching their leaves and blossoms to the sunlight. Someone, perhaps the gardener, had come. And in the tomb, the light was gone. Even the lamp that Joseph had left was cold and dark.

There was no need for it anymore.

Matthew 27:57-66

Mark 15:42 – 16:5

John 19:38-42

Stephen
AND THE JERUSALEM SANHEDRIN

The high priest of the Sanhedrin in Jerusalem looked around him slowly, nodding at those priests whom he knew well. He smoothed his long white beard and adjusted his crimson robes so that they fell just so, elegant and rich. He cleared his throat.

"This thing that has happened," he said, "is not of our doing. No charge can be laid at the feet of the Sanhedrin." He paused, looking around him, waiting for the signs of agreement. They came.

"This is a man who was accused of speaking blasphemy against our father Moses and against Almighty God himself. . . . We gathered here today — according to the law — to examine this man, this Stephen, and to see if the charges were true. It was clear to all that they were."

More nods from the gathered priests.

"If, at the end of our examination, some rose up in righteous anger to silence this man's blasphemy, we can only understand that they did what they did to stop this Stephen from betraying the faith of our fathers."

More nods.

"And one of the laws of our fathers was that the blasphemer should be set apart and killed. This is what has happened today. If there is any guilt for the spilt blood of this man, it lies with those who have turned the people away from the God of our fathers to follow their so-called Messiah."

Cheers now.

"It is the holy task of this Sanhedrin to root out the followers of Jesus of Nazareth, to stop their blasphemy, and to end the bloodshed that they provoke."

More cheers.

The high priest closed his eyes, and then turned slowly so that his back was to the rest of the Sanhedrin. He bowed his head and stretched out his arms from his sides, the long sleeves of his robes drooping like wings. He seemed to be in prayer, and slowly, one by one, the other members of the Sanhedrin left the hall. Their steps echoed; after the last one had left, it was very quiet. The high priest lowered his arms. Then he held his hands to his face.

What had he done? What had he done?

He trembled. He, the high priest of the Jerusalem Sanhedrin, trembled. What had he done?

When they had brought Stephen to be examined, he had been so sure that these followers of the carpenter were a threat. How could anyone believe that Jesus had actually risen? And yet more and more people were believing that this was true. They were abandoning their old faith, abandoning the law. It was God's will, he knew, that this should be stopped. It was God's will.

If he had to use ungodly means to perform this godly task, he decided, then that was all there was to it. It was God's will that he should do so. And so he — and others in the Sanhedrin — had used bribes, called in favors, done whatever they had to do to bring witnesses against Stephen. They had stretched the truth; otherwise they would never have been able to convict him. But even if no one had ever heard Stephen speak against Moses and blaspheme, certainly he was a follower of Jesus, and that was enough.

It was God's will. The high priest had been ready when Stephen had been brought before the Sanhedrin. And he had won.

So why was he trembling now?

Because, he knew suddenly and terribly, he had not won. He had not expected Stephen to be the kind of man that he was. He had not expected his face to look like the face of an . . . angel. He had not expected to know with a sureness deep inside him that what Stephen said was true.

"Are these charges against you true?" the high priest had asked Stephen. But Stephen had chosen not to answer this question.

"Brothers and fathers," he had said, holding out his hands to appeal not for his life but for their lives. "The God of glory appeared to our father Abraham and told him to leave his country and go to the place that the Lord God would show him. So he left, and God sent him to this land, promising him that his descendants would inherit it. And God fulfilled this promise, bringing Moses to his people and leading them up out of Egypt. He gave them this land, and gave them the law, and the tabernacle of testimony."

The members of the Sanhedrin had been as still as if they were tiles in a mosaic.

"Since that time," Stephen had continued, "this people has resisted God. Was there ever a prophet your fathers did not persecute or kill? You refuse to obey the laws God gave to you. You betrayed and murdered the Messiah that God sent."

At this the members of the Sanhedrin had leapt to their feet, screaming at Stephen. Who was he to instruct them? How dare he talk of their guilt?

But again, Stephen had not answered them. Instead he had looked up, and it had seemed as if his sight pierced the domed hall and the clouds in the sky beyond it. "Look," he had said. "Heaven is open, and Jesus is sitting at the right hand of God." He had pointed up at what he saw.

At this, three things had happened almost simultaneously. The members of the Sanhedrin had begun to scream like animals to quiet Stephen. Several had grabbed him, struck him in the face, and dragged him from the hall. And the high priest had felt his heart tremble, because he had known that what Stephen had seen was a true vision.

He heard later what had happened; the young man Saul had reported back to him before the Sanhedrin had reassembled, some still wearing bloodied cloaks. Outside the city, they had surrounded Stephen and begun to stone him to death.

"Did he say anything?" the high priest had asked his informant.

Saul had hesitated. "Yes."

"What was it?"

"'Lord Jesus, receive my spirit.'"

"Was that all?"

"No. He said, 'Lord, do not hold this sin against them.'"

"And then he died?"

"Then he died."

The high priest had motioned Saul away with a jeweled hand. This is a man who can be trusted, he had thought to himself. He may be of use later. Then he had turned to address the Sanhedrin.

But now they were gone, and he was alone. He had done God's will, he thought.

But Stephen had seen God. And he had seen Jesus. There had been a time when the high priest had yearned for a vision like that. He had hungered for it. But God had never sent it. Yet the high priest knew a few souls who had received a vision from God. He could tell that God knew them — there was something about them. And he knew that the ones so blessed received the visions because they did God's will.

The high priest, alone, turned to the tasks he had set for himself.

Acts 6:8–8:1

Ananias and Saul

IN DAMASCUS

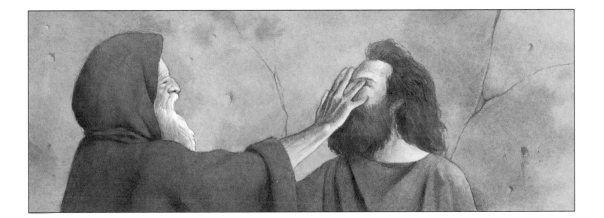

Ananias lay in his bed, his ancient eyes wide open, his heart beating quickly. Did this dream truly come from the Lord?

No. It was a nightmare meant to lead him to captivity and death. Certainly the Lord would never send him to Saul. Even the youngest disciple knew who Saul was. He had held the coats of those who murdered Stephen. He had jailed Christians from Antioch to Jerusalem. And now he had come to Damascus to jail more. The news of his arrival had sent Christians into hiding all over the city.

Certainly the Lord could not mean for Ananias to go to such a man.

And yet, the vision had been as real as any other the Lord had sent to him in his long life. Ananias let it come into his mind again, and he knew by the sweetness of the memory — never mind that the message was bitter — that this was a vision from the Lord.

"Ananias!" the Lord had called. He had recognized the voice, he remembered. There had been no question then.

"Yes, Lord," he had answered.

"Go to the house of Judas on Straight Street. There, ask for a man from Tarsus named Saul. He is praying. In a vision that I have sent to him, he has seen you come. Place your hands upon his eyes and give him back his sight."

Then the Lord's voice had left him.

Ananias continued to lie in bed for a while longer. Perhaps, he thought, this was not the same man. The Saul that the Lord spoke of was blind. But Saul of Tarsus — the one he feared so much — was not blind. He could see all too well, and he knew how to find the Christians that he was after. (With a shudder, Ananias wondered if the priests in Jerusalem had given Saul warrants for his arrest.) But this one that he was to go to, this one could not be the same man. He could not be.

But as he lay there, another vision came to him. It was the clearest vision the Lord had ever sent to him. He could see and hear and feel everything.

There was Saul, his face set and hard as iron. A hot, dry wind blew around him, scurrying the dust of the road underneath his horse's hooves and sending it in a stream back to the soldiers who clattered after him. No one spoke. The smell of heat was in the air, and the soldiers were glancing up at the sky as if they heard thunder. But Saul stared straight ahead.

Suddenly white lightning streaked from the sky and froze around Saul. He instantly fell to the ground, face down. It happened so quickly that Ananias did not see how it happened. The soldiers' horses skittered back in terror, snorting wildly, and Saul was left alone in the cloak of light, a light so bright that Ananias could not see through it. But he could hear.

"Saul! Saul! Why are you persecuting me?" It was a voice that Ananias knew well.

"Who are you, Lord?" It was Saul's voice.

"I am Jesus, whom you are persecuting."

Was that a moan from Saul?

"Get up," commanded the voice from heaven. "Go into Damascus and wait. You will be told what to do."

When the voice stopped, the light broke into glittering pieces that fell to the ground and melted away. Saul rose to one knee, one hand still on the ground; with the other he rubbed his eyes, at first slowly, then faster, back and forth, back and forth. Then he stopped.

The horses had quieted with the melting of the light. One soldier dismounted and slowly walked toward Saul. "My lord."

"I'm blind," Saul said. "Bring me into the city." The soldier, guiding Saul by the elbow, led him back to the others. When they started toward Damascus again, the soldier led Saul by the hand. Saul stared ahead at nothing.

The vision faded.

Then Ananias knew that this was indeed Saul of Tarsus. But nothing in the vision showed that Saul had changed now that he was blind. Perhaps, in his anger, he would persecute Christians even more harshly! "Lord," Ananias prayed, "I know this man. I know him by what he does. He has done much harm to the Christians in Jerusalem, and now he comes to harm those in Damascus. Must I go?"

Now the Lord spoke to Ananias a third time. "Go. This man is my instrument to bring my blessing to Israel and then to all nations."

Ananias spent the rest of that morning writing letters to those whom he loved. He wrote letters of remembrance to his family. He wrote letters of encouragement to church leaders. And he wrote letters of comfort to his close friends. Then he put on his best robe, anointed himself with oil, and left for the house of Judas on Straight Street.

As he walked, he took in everything around him, studying things as if he wanted to memorize them. The dogs snuffling through the garbage, the cries of the jewelry merchants, the smells of mutton and leeks, the shrieking of the overheated camels, the cages filled with turtledoves — these simple sights and sounds so moved him that he wondered if there had ever been a greener, sweeter day. Probably not.

It was not hard to find the way; a woman leading two young lambs pointed out the house. He knocked just once, and the door was opened by a servant. Ananias entered, touching the mezuzah with his fingertips. It seemed he was expected, for the servant led him wordlessly into a back room. And there was Saul of Tarsus. Ananias knew him.

Suddenly, all thoughts of what he had expected — the rough hands grabbing him, the sneer on Saul's face, the low insults, the quick trial — all these thoughts fell away, and Ananias wondered which of the two of them had been blinder. Here before him was the instrument of God, the one who would bring the blessing to all nations. Ananias shook his head, rubbing his own eyes. He had walked in the light of the Lord for so long, and still he could be so unseeing.

"Saul," he said simply.

Saul sat up in bed and looked in his direction with blank eyes.

"The Lord Jesus has sent me to you. The same Lord Jesus who appeared to you on the road."

Saul did not answer. He sat still, waiting for a new life to begin, waiting so eagerly that Ananias could see him shivering in the heat of the day.

"He has sent me so that you may be filled with his Spirit," Ananias finished, and leaned forward and touched his fingertips to Saul's eyes. Hard scales fell from them, and Saul sat blinking for a few moments, then stood, slowly straightening, testing what had happened. He squinted, then looked open-eyed at those around him.

"What will you do now?" asked Ananias.

Saul looked at him steadily, as if he was listening to the answer from somewhere else. "Go to the synagogue," he said simply, holding Ananias tenderly by the arm as though he were the one to guide now.

So they walked out together into the day's bright light, to see the blessings that God would prepare for them.

Acts 9:1-22